The
Complete
Food
Dehydrator
COOKBOOK

HOW TO DEHYDRATE YOUR FAVORITE FOODS USING NESCO, EXCALIBUR OR PRESTO FOOD DEHYDRATORS, INCLUDING 101 RECIPES.

Lisa Brian

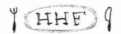

HHF Press

San Francisco

LEGAL NOTICE

The information contained in this book is for entertainment purposes only. The content represents the opinion of the author and is based on the author's personal experience and observations. The author does not assume any liability whatsoever for the use of or inability to use any or all information contained in this book, and accepts no responsibility for any loss or damages of any kind that may be incurred by the reader as a result of actions arising from the use of information in this book. Use this information at your own risk.

The author reserves the right to make any changes he or she deems necessary to future versions of the publication to ensure its accuracy.

DO YOU LIKE FREE BOOKS?

Every month we release a new book, and we offer it to our current readers first...absolutely free! This helps us get early feedback before launching a book, and lets you stock your shelf full of interesting and valuable books for free!

Some recent titles include:

- The Complete Vegetable Spiralizer Cookbook

- The Cast Iron Recipe Cookbook

- 101 Crepe Recipe

To receive this month's free book, just go to

www.healthyhappyfoodie.org/e1-freebooks

Table of Contents

CHAPTER 1: WHY YOU NEED THIS BOOK   10

CHAPTER 2 WHAT IS DEHYDRATING?   14

CHAPTER 3: BENEFITS OF DEHYDRATING   18

CHAPTER 4: THE BEST ELECTRIC DEHYDRATORS   25

CHAPTER 5: HOW TO DEHYDRATE   31

CHAPTER 6: HOW TO CHOOSE THE BEST FOODS FOR DEHYDRATION   38

CHAPTER 7: DEHYDRATING AND STORING SAFELY   43

CHAPTER 8: PRO-DEHYDRATING TIPS   45

CHAPTER 9: HOW TO USE THIS BOOK   50

CHAPTER 10: FRUIT RECIPES   52

    3-Ingredient Banana Raisin Cookies   53

    Apple-Cherry-Apricot Fruit Leather   54

    Apple Pie Leather   55

    Asian Pear and Ginger Treats   56

    Banana Cocoa Leather   57

    Cherry Coconut Almond Cookies   58

    Chewy Lemony Treats   59

    Energy Balls   60

    Fruit Sprinkles   61

    Goji Berry Leather   62

Honey Banana Walnut Chips   63

Nothing But Fruit Bars   64

"PB&G": Peanut Butter, Banana and Graham Cracker
Cookie Bars   65

Raspberry Banana Fruit Leather   66

Raw Fig Balls   67

Spiced Apple Chips   68

Spicy Strawberry Fruit Leather   69

Strawberry-Pineapple Fruit Leather   70

Sweet and Sour Cranberries   71

Sweet "Caramel Apples"   72

Sweet Potato- Cinnamon Leather   73

Tangy Dried Mangos   74

Tropical Pineapple Crisps   75

Vanilla-Apricot Slices   76

Watermelon Candy Slices   77

CHAPTER 11: VEGETABLE RECIPES   **78**

Brussels Sprouts "Croutons"   79

Cauliflower Poppers   80

Crunchy Asian Green Beans   81

Crunchy Kale Chips   82

Fall Carrot Chips   83

Herbed Sweet Potato Chips   84

Hot & Spicy Potato Sticks   85

Indian Cauliflower   86

Lemon Pepper Yellow Squash Rounds   87

Marinated Eggplant   88

Mediterranean Style "Sun-Dried" Tomatoes   89

Moroccan Carrot Crunch   90

Parmesan Cucumber Chips   91

Ranch Brussels Sprout Skins   92

Root Vegetable Medley   94

Salt & Pepper Vinegar Zucchini Chips   95

Salt and Vinegar Cucumber Chips   96

Smoked Collard Green Chips   97

Smoky Sweet Potato Chips   98

Spinach Balls   99

Sour Cream and Onion Potato Chips   100

Southwestern Style Cauliflower Popcorn   102

Sweet Kale Chips   103

Sweet and Savory Beet Rounds   104

Tex-Mex Green Beans   105

Vegan Broccoli Crisps   106

CHAPTER 12: MEAT RECIPES   **107**

Asian Jerky   108

BBQ Jerky Strips   109

Bold Beef Jerky 110

Boozy Jerky 111

Garlicky Beef Jerky 112

Marinated Jerky 113

Orange Flavored Beef Jerky 114

Pastrami Jerky 116

Salmon Jerky 117

"Smoked" Turkey 118

Smokey Mexican Jerky 119

Spiced "Hamburger" Jerky 120

Spiced Turkey Jerky 121

Spicy Harissa Flavored Jerky 122

Sweet and Spicy Venison or Beef Jerky 124

Thai Sweet Chili Jerky 125

Teriyaki Jerky 126

CHAPTER 13: GRAINS, NUTS AND SEEDS RECIPES **127**

Apple and Nut "Raw" Cereal 128

Almond Cranberry Cookies 130

Asian-Inspired Nuts 131

Apple Cinnamon Graham Cookies 132

Banana Breakfast Crepes 134

Basic "Soaked Nuts" 135

Blueberry Nut Bars 136

Blueberry Oat Pancakes 137

Caramelized Almonds 138

Chocolate Covered Walnuts 139

Classic Oatmeal Raisin Cookies 140

Coconut Butter Macaroons 141

Flax Seed Crackers 142

Fruit n' Nut Balls 143

Fruit & Nut Clusters 144

"Graham Crackers" 146

Macadamia-Sage Crackers 147

Hazelnut Lemon Crackers 148

Mint-Scented Chocolate Chip Cookies 150

Orange-Scented Granola with Dried Blueberries 151

Parmesan Black Pepper Flax Crackers 152

Pepita Crackers 153

"Raw" Cheesy Thyme Crackers 154

"Raw" Granola 155

Savory Onion and Garlic Crisps 156

Savory Trail Mix 157

Seasoned Sunflower Seeds 158

Sesame Seed Crisps 159

Spicy Cashews 160

Sweet and Salty Pumpkin Seeds 161

Sweet Cocoa Chia Bars 162

Wasabi Sesame Crackers   164

Sundried Tomato Flax Crackers   166

NEXT STEPS...   **167**

ABOUT THE AUTHOR   **168**

DON'T FORGET TO REGISTER FOR FREE BOOKS...   **169**

WHY YOU NEED THIS BOOK

Discover A New Method Of Food Preparation And Conservation

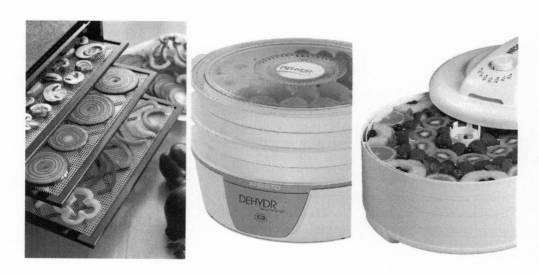

In the next few pages, you will be introduced to the unique benefits of dehydrating food. A dehydrator can produce affordable and easy-to-prepare foods with minimal time and effort. Using a dehydrator allows you to transform ingredients into delicious and novel snacks and meals. Have fun experimenting with a wide array of foods. Your excess ingredients will no longer go to waste. With proper storage techniques, dehydrated foods can last for months. Dehydration will quickly become your go-to process for transforming raw ingredients into all types of ready-to-eat foods!

Learn How To Choose The Best Dehydrator For Your Needs

This book provides detailed comparisons of the most popular electric dehydrators on the market. Learn about the major features that distinguish the top selling dehydrator brands from one another to determine which machine is the most suitable for you. You will learn about factors to consider when choosing the right dehydrator, such as: the quantities of food you plan to prepare; whether you have adequate shelf space; how much you value efficiency and precise electronic controls in your machine; what type of heating and fan system you prefer; and what your budget guidelines are.

Learn How To Choose Ingredients For Delicious Dehydrated Foods

In these pages, you will not only discover the wide array of foods that can be dehydrated with your machine, you will also read about how to choose ingredients wisely to yield the best food products. This book will inform you about which fruits, vegetables, herbs, meats and grains are the most delicious and appropriate for dehydration, as well as the foods that do not maintain their flavor and quality after dehydration.

Learn How To Dehydrate Safely And Effectively

Find out how to create healthy dehydrated foods safely, while retaining the ingredient's inherent freshness. The safety guidelines in this book describe how to maintain proper temperature and time controls for dehydration. You will get detailed advice on choosing the right packaging and environment for dehydrated food and maximizing the shelf life of your foods.

How To Get The Best Results When Dehydrating Your Food

Use this book to achieve the best results from your dehydrator! Discover the tricks and tips that dehydrating pros rely upon to produce varied foods of the highest quality. Go beyond the basic guidelines for preparation and storage in the machine owner's manual. This informative section will reveal how to best to ensure your food dehydrates properly, stays flavorful and is safe for consumption for months to come.

101 Delicious Recipes In One Handy Book

Look no further for a comprehensive guide to the best recipes for dehydrating food. Learn how to make dried fruit snacks and fruit leather in various flavors. See how versatile vegetables and beef can be for creating crispy chips and gourmet jerkies.

Discover the various food preparations that are possible when you dehydrate or sprout nuts, seeds and grains. These recipes are specifically designed for use in conjunction with your electric dehydrator to create delicious, nutritious, simple-to-execute foods.

WHAT IS DEHYDRATING?

Basic Dehydration Process

Dehydration, or the process of extracting moisture from food, is one of the oldest methods of food preparation.

While the sun or a conventional oven can get the job done, an electric dehydrator is the most efficient way to dehydrate foods. Electric dehydrators use low heat and air flow to remove food's natural moisture. The advantage of an electric dehydrator is that it is quicker and less laborious than other methods, such as oven-drying. Another benefit of this method is that a wide array of foods can be dehydrated.

Dehydration Is An Inexpensive, Quick Simple Way To Eat Produce, Meat And Grains

Compared to many other specialized culinary gadgets, dehydrators are relatively affordable. Once you purchase your dehydrator, there are no other expensive ingredients or accessories required to operate your machine. Similarly, most recipes for dehydrated foods require just minutes to prepare. There are rarely complicated steps to follow. All you need to do is prep your particular ingredient and the dehydrating machine does all the rest!

Dehydration Is A Great Alternative To Canning Or Freezing

Canning and freezing are traditional methods of preserving fresh foods. Dehydration similarly preserves food from season to season but has certain additional benefits. Foremost, dehydration is superior to canning or freezing with respect to the retention of nutrients. Dehydration also preserves flavor better than canning and freezing and results in a higher quality product.

Dehydration Produces Portable Food That Requires Minimal Space And Refrigeration.

Dehydrated foods are compact and store easily in a pantry. They are ideal for meals and snacks to be eaten on-the-go, whether at school, at work or while traveling. Most dehydrated foods don't require cooling or heating and can sustain short-term exposure to various temperatures.

At home, dehydrated foods will not monopolize your refrigerator and freezer space. You will never need to carry cumbersome coolers and thermoses again when you take along dehydrated snack foods.

Creates Versatile Food Products

Dehydration will provide you with a plethora of food options. Simply prepared, dehydrated produce is optimal for healthy snacking. Dehydrated vegetables and herbs can be building blocks for healthy soups, stews, sauces, omelettes and crepes. Assemble herb blends to create herb-infused oils and butters when fresh herbs are unavailable. Dehydrated foods have a variety of textures from crunchy and crispy to soft and chewy, and often retain their shape and texture better than other methods of preservation.

BENEFITS OF DEHYDRATING

Yields Healthy, Preservative-Free And Chemical-Free Foods

Research has shown the importance of eating a diet consisting primarily of unprocessed, whole foods.

Dehydration uses whole foods. When making dehydrated foods, there is no need to add chemicals, preservatives or excess sodium to ensure freshness or enhance taste. Both are maintained as a result of the natural process of dehydration. You know exactly what goes into your food and are not exposed to ingredients you cannot decipher. Moreover, although many of us are aware of the benefits of fresh, whole foods, we are often faced with the dilemma that these foods stay fresh for only a limited time. Dehydrating allows you to enjoy foods with a prolonged shelf life without the addition of chemicals.

Incorporating dehydrated food into your diet can also expand your raw food repertoire. Dehydrators are widely utilized by adherents of the raw food movement. When applying temperatures under 118° F, foods are not subjected to the higher temperatures required for canning or cooking.

Retains Food's Nutritional Value

According to studies, raw plant cells provide the most balanced nutrition profile. Dehydrated foods leave vitamins, such as A and C, and minerals, such as potassium and magnesium, intact. Dehydrated foods are not only nutritionally superior to packaged, processed foods, but in many respects they are preferable to foods preserved through other methods.

Dehydration results in only a 3-5% loss in nutrients. By comparison, canning entails a 60-80% depletion in nutrients while freezing normally results in a 40-60% decrease in nutrients.

In addition, certain foods, such as nuts, seeds and grains, are believed to attain a nutritional advantage when they are soaked and dehydrated or sprouted. Soaking raw nuts and seeds and then dehydrating them for later use helps to neutralize enzyme inhibitors, makes proteins more accessible and increases the potency of certain vitamins.

Preserves Surplus Food For Future Use

Dehydration is the most economical way to use raw ingredients. Once you have purchased your electric dehydrator, preserving food for future use is simple and affordable. If you have an abundance of fruits or vegetables from your own garden, you never need to dispose of that excess produce. You can enjoy seasonal produce all year round by dehydrating your favorite summer fruits.

Similarly, you can make more budget-friendly decisions for your family by purchasing produce or meat at reduced cost and dehydrating it for future use. Buying in bulk will save you time and money, and allow you to build up a reserve for future enjoyment.

Budget-Friendly Alternative To Expensive Grocery Store Products

Dehydration machines are capable of creating large quantities of food with minimal effort. Finally, you have a replacement for trendy and costly pre-made dehydrated food snacks.

Producing your own healthy fruit, vegetable and meat snacks means that you do not need to resort to feeding your children unhealthy snacks simply because they are often the cheaper option.

Given the variety of foods you can create, grocery store visits may not be as frequent.

Extended Shelf Life And A Cinch To Store

Dehydrated foods last for several months depending on the type of food you prepare. For example, certain low moisture herbs have extensive shelf lives.

Dehydrated foods don't require special storage materials. It is not necessary to purchase expensive equipment for storage, or refrigeration and freezing apparatuses to maintain the food's freshness. Jars with tight-fitting lids and a dark, cool area to keep them are all you need for proper storage. With these handling routines, food remains preserved and delicious for months.

Makes Healthy Eating Accessible And Convenient

One of the main impediments to consuming healthier foods is a lack of knowledge about how to prepare them. Often people think that they need to purchase ready-to-eat food products to maintain a nutritionally rich diet. With a dehydrator, healthy foods can be prepared right at home. You can choose produce directly from your garden for dehydration. It can be as simple as preparing a vegetable salad with your garden's produce, but much more interesting and varied. Many electric dehydrators have expedited drying times so food can be eaten promptly.

Eating Dehydrated Foods Is Optimal For Weight Loss

In addition to the overall health benefits of dehydration, dehydrated foods can play a role in achieving weight loss. Dehydrated foods do not contain added sugar or artificial sweeteners, which are primary contributors to obesity. Dehydrated foods are naturally low in fat and high in fiber. Fiber-rich foods are essential to a well-balanced diet and may help in the prevention of heart disease, diabetes, certain cancers and digestive problems.

High fiber foods, such as fruits, vegetables, beans, and whole grain products, also assist in long-term weight loss. Studies have demonstrated that because fiber swells in your stomach when it absorbs liquid, eating fiber-rich foods gives an individual the feeling of being satiated and reduces overall calorie consumption. Dehydrated food, in particular, hinders the natural triggers that signal fullness because of the food's resulting compact size. In addition, dehydrated foods take more time to digest due to their dryness and complexity.

THE BEST ELECTRIC DEHYDRATORS

Factors To Consider When Choosing The Best Dehydrator For Your Needs

Dehydrators operate by using a heating source, fan and vents to circulate air and remove moisture from foods. The heat captures the moisture from the food and releases it into the dehydrator. The fan pushes moisture to the vents to be discharged outside the dehydrator. There are several main features that distinguish the top-selling dehydrators from one another. These features include the machine's air flow system, size and capacity, and temperature settings and controls.

Air Flow

The air flow mechanism in a dehydrating machine can produce either horizontal or vertical air flow. With vertical air flow units, the fan is located at the top or bottom of the machine. As a result, the machine may not produce uniformly dehydrated foods as the items closest to the fan will tend to dry first. Horizontal air flow units have rear mounted fans. Horizontal units are generally preferred for two reasons: heat is more evenly dispersed throughout the unit, thereby creating a more consistent product. Second, these units minimize the likelihood that different flavors will get mixed during the dehydration process.

Size Considerations

Electric dehydrators generally come in two forms: stacked dehydrators and box and shelf dehydrators. Stacked dehydrators are made up of racks that are stacked on top of each other. The fan is located at the bottom and the air circulates vertically.

Box and shelf dehydrators are comprised of an outer-shell and trays, and operate like electric ovens. The fan is located in the rear and disperses air horizontally. These higher capacity dehydrators are bulkier and pricier than the stacked variety.

Temperature Settings and Controls.

Many of the more popular brands of dehydrators have adjustable temperature settings that can be helpful in maintaining an even temperature throughout the dehydration process. This feature allows you to dehydrate a variety of foods that require different temperatures. The generally recommended setting for herbs is about 95 degrees F while beef jerky is 155 degrees F; thus, an adjustable setting option is necessary to accommodate both these ingredients.

Popular Dehydrators

Three of the most popular dehydrators on the market are manufactured by Nesco, Excalibur and Presto. This section will address some of the advantages and disadvantages of each machine.

Nesco

Nesco is an excellent machine for beginners and ideal for average to moderate use. The Nesco's unique drying system and fan position allow food to dry uniformly, which is one of the most frequently cited benefits of this appliance. The Nesco dehydrator's vertical air flow system pushes air down the outside chamber and allows air to be evenly dispersed.

The distribution of air horizontally eliminates the need to rotate trays. In addition, the Nesco dehydrator has adjustable temperature controls and expands to add more trays if necessary. The Nesco SnackMaster Pro Food Dehydrator FD75-A, one of the most popular Nesco brand models, is an affordable option at just under $100.

The main drawbacks of the Nesco FD75-A dehydrator is that is does not contain a timer or an on/off switch. The user would need to closely monitor the foods during the dehydration process and then shut off the machine when the food is sufficiently dehydrated.

Excalibur

The Excalibur dehydrator is the ideal machine for large capacity dehydration and has some of the most sophisticated features on the market. The Excalibur 3926TB 9-Tray Dehydrator provides 15 square feet of drying space and includes an automated timer and adjustable temperature settings.

The machine contains a drying system with fan-forced, horizontal air flow that ensures even distribution of heat and air and eliminates the need to rotate trays. This mechanism produces consistently high quality results on a large variety of foods. The trays and door on this box-style model are easily removable.

Two of the biggest disadvantages of this model are its size and price. This model is priced between $200 and $250, but considering its superior temperature control system, you might determine that the Excalibur provides the best value. The size of the machine is an additional consideration. To accommodate the shape and large capacity of this dehydrator, you will need a fair amount of counter space in your kitchen. Some users have also indicated that the dehydration process for this machine is somewhat lengthy.

Presto

The Presto dehydrator earned high ratings for the simplicity of its features. Unlike the Nesco and Excalibur, the Presto has a vertical airflow system so that heat commences from the bottom and moves upwards in a vertical direction. The Presto dehydrator is compact, making it a suitable size for most kitchen countertops and allowing for easy clean-up. The machine also contains a transparent top cover to allow you to monitor the drying process. Some of the models contain timers and temperature controls, while others do not. The Presto dehydrator is budget friendly, costing under $50.

The most significant drawback of the Presto dehydrator is the noise it produces. Certain models lack an on/off switch and require unplugging the machine to turn it off. Similarly, the lack of a temperature control gauge in some machines may result in improperly dehydrated foods.

HOW TO DEHYDRATE

Preparing Fruits For Dehydration

Most dehydrating machines, no matter which brand or model you choose, are user-friendly. The first step in preparing fruits for the dehydration machine is selecting high-quality fruits.

Fruit should be fresh and at the peak of ripeness. Once you pick or purchase your produce, thoroughly wash it and discard any bruised or damaged pieces. Fruits may need to be peeled, cored or pitted, depending on the particular fruit you are handling.

After fruit has been peeled and sliced, it is advisable to apply a pre-treatment to maintain the color and freshness of the produce. Once certain fruits, such as apples, pears and peaches are sliced, their exposure to air initiates a chemical process called oxidation that results in discolored flesh. Using an antioxidant will temporarily halt the enzyme action and prevent further damage to the texture, flavor and appearance of the fruit. To make this solution, combine a small amount of ascorbic acid (1-2 tsp.) with one cup of water and coat the fruit evenly with the liquid.

Preparing Vegetables For Dehydration

When preparing your vegetables for dehydration, be sure to select high-quality, unblemished vegetables.

Particularly for certain vegetables such as root vegetables and potatoes, make sure they are thoroughly scrubbed and cleaned prior to dehydration. Similar to fruits, vegetables should be sliced thinly and uniformly for the best results.

Nearly all vegetables should be blanched first. Blanching vegetables halts enzyme action and thereby preserves the color and flavor of the food over time. Because some nutrients may be lost during the blanching process, place the vegetables in boiling water only for the required length of time.

After the vegetables are submerged in ice cold water, carefully dry the foods prior to placing them on trays.   Note that a small number of vegetables, like mushrooms and onions, do not need to be blanched prior to dehydration.

Preparing Meat For Dehydration

Dehydrated meats are delicious and simple to prepare, but do warrant special handling instructions. Only lean meats in excellent condition should be utilized for making jerky. When using ground meat for jerky, it should be at least 93% lean.

All other meat should have its fat thoroughly trimmed prior to slicing. You might consider applying a marinade beforehand to flavor the meat. If so, keep marinated meats in the refrigerator or freezer before placing them in the dehydrator. After removing the meat from the refrigerator, blot its surface thoroughly to remove excess moisture and place on dehydrator trays. As always, raw meat should be kept away from other foods, and all surfaces and utensils that come into contact with raw meat should be thoroughly cleaned.

After using the dehydrator, experts recommend heating dried meat strips for ten minutes in a 275° F oven or for a longer time at a lower temperature. This additional step reduces any residual chance of contamination by eliminating pathogens, and also produces the most traditional style of jerky with respect to taste and texture.

Preparing Grains, Nuts, Beans And Seeds For Dehydration

Nuts, seeds, beans and grains can all be dehydrated using a similar two-step process. First, these foods must be soaked in a water solution. Soaking deactivates anti-nutrients, stimulates nutrients such as iron, potassium and magnesium, and is beneficial to your digestive system. Soak nuts or seeds in a salt brine solution for 12-18 hours. Add ½ tsp. high-quality sea salt for every cup of water. Since wet nuts and seeds are not appealing to most people, you can place the nuts in the dehydrator to create a delicious, crunchy, ready to eat snack. After soaking for the recommended time, drain the water and proceed with instructions for your dehydrating machine.

Using Your Dehydrator Machine

Once the fruits, vegetables, herbs, meat, nuts or grains have been prepped, spread them in thin layers without overlapping on the drying trays. Turn on the dehydrating machine and set the temperature. Drying times vary depending on the dehydrator model you own and the food you are dehydrating. Most dehydrators contain guides that provide recommended temperatures and times for dehydrating specific foods.

In general, it is recommended that fruits and vegetables be dried at 130°-140° F. Meats and fish should be dehydrated at the highest temperature setting on your machine, which is typically between 145°-155° F. When dehydrating meats, it is necessary to use dehydrator models with adjustable temperature controls to ensure a product that is safe for consumption. Dried herbs require a temperature not exceeding 90° F, as aromatic oils in herbs are sensitive to high heat. Nuts, seeds and grains, which also have a high oil content, dry optimally at 90°-100° F.

Determining Food Readiness

Foods should always be tested for adequate dehydration before removal. Many factors determine the length of time necessary to dehydrate foods, such as the temperature, humidity, type of food, amount of food on the tray, size of the food pieces, and total quantity of food in the machine.

In general, meats should be dehydrated to 20% moisture content, fruits to 10% and vegetables to about 5%. You can analyze the appearance and texture of foods for signs of readiness. It is important to test only a few pieces at a time and allow them to cool before determining whether they are ready.

Checking food for readiness is largely a matter of assessing its structure. Fruits should be pliable, but not totally brittle. Test fruits by cutting them in half; if you cannot squeeze out any moisture, then the fruit is fully dehydrated. Vegetables, however, should be brittle when they are done. Test vegetables by hitting them with a hammer to see if they shatter.

Most fully dehydrated vegetables should break into pieces. Certain vegetables, however, will retain a pliable and leathery texture upon complete dehydration. These include mushrooms, green peppers and squash. To test jerky, bend one piece and see how pliable it is. The meat should bend, but not snap completely like a dry stick. The jerky should present as dark brown to black in color once it is fully dehydrated. Herbs are considered dried when they crumble easily. The stems of the herb should bend and break with little effort.

HOW TO CHOOSE THE BEST FOODS FOR DEHYDRATION

Categories Of Foods Ideal For Dehydration

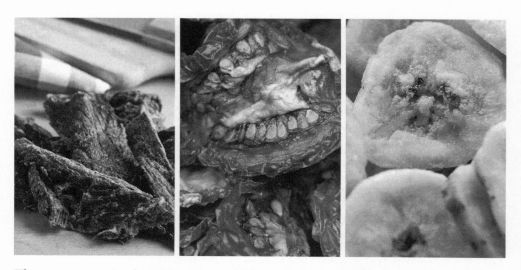

There are particular categories of food that are optimal for dehydration. These are: fruits, vegetables and herbs; meat, fish and poultry; and grains, nuts and seeds.

Many other types of ingredients are not suitable for dehydration. For example, foods that are high in fat, such as avocados, go rancid fairly quickly when dehydrated.

Most Fruits Dehydrate Well

A wide array of fruits provide excellent choices for delicious dehydrated foods. In particular apples, apricots, plums, bananas and tomatoes are optimal for your dehydrating machine. Certain fruits dehydrate well in whole form, such as berries, grapes and cherries. Fruits are relatively forgiving as food choices for dehydration. The key to great results is following the instructions for preparing and pre-treating fruits in **Chapter 5** (How to dehydrate).

Certain Vegetables Are More Suitable For Dehydration

Many vegetables are delicious and nutritious in their dehydrated forms, such as peas, green beans, potatoes, celery, beets and carrots. However, certain vegetables are better candidates than others for dehydration due to their low moisture content. High moisture vegetables should not be used for dehydration. When the moisture content of the vegetable is too high in its raw state, it does not retain its flavor and its structure becomes compromised once it is dehydrated.

Nearly All Herbs Can Be Dehydrated

Most herbs are naturally low in moisture. Herbs such as tarragon, thyme and sage dehydrate well due to their low-moisture content. Many herbs, such as oregano, rosemary and thyme, retain their flavor in a dried rather than fresh state, and may actually be preferable in certain recipes. In general, the key to successfully dehydrating herbs is largely a function of dehydrating the herb as quickly as possible at a fairly low temperature.

Optimal Meats For Dehydration

High fat cuts of beef cannot be dehydrated properly and are not safe for long term storage. Therefore, always choose the leanest cuts of meat. Freeze or partially freeze meat first to create the most uniform slices for beef jerky. For other proteins, such as pork and wild game, the meat must be frozen to kill the Trichinella parasite before it is sliced and marinated. While freezing does not eradicate potential parasites from the meat, it kills the parasite so that meat can be safely dehydrated. Raw poultry is not recommended for making jerky due to its flavor and texture after it has been dehydrated.

Refer To The Chart Below For Suggestions For Some Of The Best Foods To Dehydrate.

Fruits

Apples	Figs	Nectarines
Apricots	Grapes	Oranges
Bananas	Kiwi	Peaches
Berries {all types}	Lemons	Pears
Cherries	Mangoes	Pineapples
Cranberries	Melon	Plums

Vegetables

Beans {green}	Corn	Peppers
Beets	Eggplant	Potatoes
Broccoli	Garlic	Squash
Carrots	Mushrooms	Tomatoes
Cauliflower	Onions	
Celery	Peas	

Herbs

Anise	Dill	Parsley
Basil	Fennel	Rosemary
Chives	Garlic	Sage
Cilantro	Marjoram	Tarragon
Coriander	Mint	Thyme
Cumin	Oregano	

Meats

Flank Steak	Ground Round	Pork
Round Steak	Lean Fish	

Grains / Nuts / Seeds

Almonds	Pecans	Chickpeas
Buckwheat	Pinenuts	Green peas
Cashews	Walnuts	Lentils
Hazelnuts	Sunflower seeds	Quinoa

DEHYDRATING AND STORING SAFELY

The Dehydration Process Naturally Protects Food

The process of dehydration inhibits bacterial growth by removing nearly all moisture from the ingredient. In addition, dehydration slows enzyme action without deactivating them, which ensures that food is better protected from spoiling.

Food Must Be Dehydrated To The Right Temperature

When dehydrating foods, the drying mechanism must be hot enough to release moisture, but not hot enough to initiate the cooking process.

Dehydrating food to the proper temperature prevents the proliferation of mold, yeast and bacteria. Only by maintaining adequate temperature controls can you ensure the safety of dehydrated food and prolong its freshness. See Chapter 5, How to Dehydrate: Using Your Dehydrator Machine for information on proper dehydrating temperatures for various food groups.

Provide Ideal Conditions

Once food is properly dried and cooled, it must be stored in air - tight containers. Packaging the food in small quantities is ideal since you are less likely to contaminate portions that are not used immediately. It is important to package the food tightly and squeeze out any excess air if you are using re-sealable plastic bags.

Containers should be placed in a cool, dark, moisture-free environment. A closed kitchen cupboard is an ideal place to store dehydrated food containers. Maintain a moderate temperature to preserve the freshness and color of foods.

Most dried foods can be stored for six months to one year. If recommendations are followed, vegetables can be safely stored for about 6 months. Fruits and herbs will generally remain useable for up to one year. Jerky can keep for one to two months at room temperature and in the freezer for six months or longer.

Alternatively, to extend the shelf life of jerky, you can use vacuum packaging. Dehydrated nuts and seeds can remain in the fridge for several weeks. Periodically check dehydrated foods for moisture. If moisture is detected, it is advisable to dehydrate and package the food again. If there are any signs of mold, the food should be immediately discarded.

PRO-DEHYDRATING TIPS

Once you have mastered the basic processes for dehydration and preservation and chosen the best foods for dehydrating, use the tips in this section to help you dehydrate like an expert!

Thinly Sliced Fruits And Vegetables Are Optimal For Dehydration

When dehydrating fruits and vegetables, properly slicing the produce significantly affects the quality of the food. Uniformly slicing the fruits and vegetables will ensure even cooking time for all components and reduce the likelihood of having to discard undercooked portions. To ensure evenly sliced vegetables, it is advisable to use a mandoline. Thinly cut fruits and vegetables also dehydrate more rapidly.

Post-Treatment Of Dehydrated Fruits

To permanently prevent the discoloration of fruit once it has been dehydrated, exposing the fruit to sulfur is recommended. Sulfur is not harmful in the small amounts necessary for these purposes and has the added benefits of retaining Vitamins A and C and discouraging the growth of microbes. Submerge fruit in a sulfite solution immediately after it has been dehydrated in much the same way you would prepare and apply the antioxidant solution.

Dissolve one Tbsp. sodium bisulfite in one gallon of water. Soak the fruit for five-ten minutes and rinse. Sodium bisulfite is usually available in drugstores and wine stores. Sulfating is not recommended for individuals on sodium-free diets.

Special Considerations For Tough, Waxy Fruits

The skins of certain fruits, such as blueberries, cherries and grapes, are tough and waxy. As such, they should be "cracked" prior to dehydration. To crack the skins and allow the interior moisture to come to the surface, blanch the fruit by placing it in boiling water for 30 to 60 seconds and then submerge it promptly in very cold water.

Dehydrating Vegetables Wisely

Certain vegetables are more amenable to the dehydration process than others. For example, if you want to preserve asparagus, freezing might be a better option than dehydrating to maintain flavor.

Certain vegetables, such as mushrooms, need to be dried very well after they are washed since they easily soak up moisture. Combinations of vegetables can be dried simultaneously, but refrain from drying vegetables with strong odors alongside mild flavored vegetables as the latter will retain the odors. For example, always dehydrate garlic and onions by themselves to prevent their flavors from comingling with other vegetables.

Marinating Meats For To Enhance Their Safety

In addition to the safety measures discussed in this book for dehydrating proteins (see Chapter 5: How to dehydrate: Preparing meat for dehydration), marinating the meat prior to dehydration has shown to be somewhat effective in preventing the growth of pathogens. The spices and nitrites commonly found in marinades and dry seasoning mixes play a role in the destruction of pathogens. See the recipes section of this book for marinades.

Texture And Appearance Are Reliable Clues To Food Safety

Although most electric dehydrators contain adjustable temperature controls, it is advisable to periodically test the food by hand while it is in the process of dehydrating. With increased exposure to dehydration, you will begin to gauge when food is ready from analyzing its texture and appearance. To quickly and easily determine whether food is completely dehydrated, place a few pieces in a plastic bag and seal it. If you notice any condensation forming, the dehydration process is not complete and you should continue to dehydrate it.

Thoroughly Moisture-Proof Your Dehydrated Food

Storing dehydrated food in a moisture-proof environment is the key to its flavor, appearance and longevity. There are steps you can take to create the proper conditions for dehydrated food. First, choose lids with rubber gaskets.

If you use glass jars, place them in an area free of sunlight so as not to discolor the foods or choose colored jars. Place cotton balls in jars as they will absorb any residual moisture. Alternatively, you can place foods in Ziplock bags with firm seals.

To Rehydrate Or Not To Rehydrate?

Many dehydrated products are consumed in their dried states, but others might benefit from rehydration. Particularly when using dried vegetables and herbs as components for soups, stews, casseroles or other cooked food preparations, rehydrating, or refreshing, is advisable. The process of rehydrating simply entails soaking or cooking the dried food until volume is adequately restored.

Both dehydrated and rehydrated foods are nutritionally dense and safe to consume assuming proper preparation techniques were followed. However, foods should be rehydrated only when they are ready to be used; storing rehydrated foods introduces microbes that compromise the safety and quality of the food.

HOW TO USE THIS BOOK

To get started on adding dehydrated foods to your regular diet, scan the topical bullet points in each of the eight previous chapters. For a comprehensive guide to dehydration, begin with Chapter 7 for an overview of safety concerns. This chapter will provide you with information you should know beforehand to ensure that you are preparing and consuming food as directed by the manufacturer and in accordance with relevant safety standards. Then turn to Chapter 4 to review the pros and cons of top selling dehydrators.

Many readers will have already purchased a dehydrating machine prior to reading this book, but this side-by-side comparison will highlight the distinct features of each brand and serve as a guide if you are still contemplating which machine to purchase.

Once you have chosen your electric dehydrator and are generally familiar with safety procedures, you can learn about the most suitable foods for this cooking technique. Chapter 6 provides helpful tips on the easiest and tastiest foods, as well as the least successful options, for dehydration. Begin by choosing a few ingredients and familiarize yourself with the techniques for dehydration found in Chapter 5. Then review pro-dehydrating tips in Chapter 8. These suggestions and observations will assist you in producing the highest-quality foods and applying the best conservation methods. Finally, scan the recipe section for ideas and instructions for preparing delicious dehydrated foods (Chapter 10).

FRUIT RECIPES

3-Ingredient Banana Raisin Cookies

You probably already have the ingredients for these easy, vegan cookies in your pantry. Take your overripe bananas and use your dehydrator to create these tasty treats. The texture of these cookies should be soft and chewy, not crisp, so do not over-dehydrate.

Nutritional Info (per 1-oz serving): *Calories: 104, Sodium: 33 mg, Dietary Fiber: 1.4 g, Total Fat: 4.1 g, Total Carbs: 16.3 g, Protein: 1.3 g.*

Ingredients:

1 very ripe banana, mashed

1 cup raisins

1 cup sweetened flake coconut

Instructions:

- Rehydrate raisins for 20 minutes in warm water.
- Combine banana, raisins and coconut in a food processor until a paste forms.
- Dehydrate for 6-8 hours at 110 degrees. Flip mixture over and dehydrate for another 6 hours.

Apple-Cherry-Apricot Fruit Leather

The tartness of cherries and granny smith apples combine with sweet apricots to make a refreshing fruit leather. Besides adding sweetness, honey enhances the soft, chewy texture of the fruit leather.

Nutritional Info (per 1-oz serving): Calories: 42, Sodium: 2 mg, Dietary Fiber: 0.6 g, Total Fat: 0.1 g, Total Carbs: 10.8 g, Protein: 0.2 g.

Ingredients:

1 cup peeled apricots, sliced into chunks

1 cup granny smith apples, peeled, cored and cut into small chunks

½ cup cherries, stems discarded and pitted

1-2 Tbsp. honey

Instructions:

- Puree apricots, apples and cherries in a food processor. Add honey and pulse.
- Pour mixture onto fruit leather sheets.
- Set the temperature to 135 degrees.
- Dry for 8-10 hours, or until leathery to touch.

Apple Pie Leather

This delicious fruit leather tastes just like everyone's fall favorite - apple pie! Remember to lightly oil your trays for speedy cleanup. If you don't have apple pie spice, use some combination of nutmeg, cloves and cardamom, depending on your preferences.

Nutritional Info (per 1-oz serving): *Calories: 20, Sodium: 1 mg, Dietary Fiber: 0.6 g, Total Fat: 0.1 g, Total Carbs: 5.4 g, Protein: 0.1 g.*

Ingredients:

6 apples, peeled, cored and chopped

1 cup coconut milk

2 cups applesauce

¼ cup honey

1 tsp. ground cinnamon

1 tsp. apple pie spice

2 Tbsp. finely chopped raisins

Instructions:

- Place all ingredients in a food processor and pulse once or twice.
- Spread mixture on greased fruit leather dehydrator sheets.
- Dehydrate for 8-24 hours at 135 degrees.
- Cut into strips and roll into cylinders.

Asian Pear and Ginger Treats

The refreshing taste of Asian pear combined with the sharpness of ginger work together to create a sophisticated snack. Be sure to finely grate your ginger as not to overpower the subtle flavor of these pears.

Nutritional Info (per 1-oz serving): *Calories: 18, Sodium: 0 mg, Dietary Fiber: 0.8 g, Total Fat: 0 g, Total Carbs: 4.9 g, Protein: 0.1 g.*

Ingredients:

6 medium sized Asian pears, peeled, pitted and cored

1 ½ tsp. honey

4 Tbsp. warm water

1 small knob of ginger, finely grated

Instructions:

- In a bowl, mix honey and ginger. Add the water and mix well.

- Slice Asian pears into uniform slices, around ¼ inch thick. Arrange pear slices onto dehydrator tray and brush with a thin layer of ginger-honey mixture.

- Dehydrate for 9-12 hours at 135 degrees.

Banana Cocoa Leather

The addition of unsweetened cocoa makes this fruit leather a guilt-free dessert. You can use a small amount of either corn syrup or maple syrup. But add the sweetener slowly; the dehydration process concentrates flavors so a little goes a long way.

Nutritional Info (per 1-oz serving): *Calories: 42, Sodium: 1 mg, Dietary Fiber: 2 g, Total Fat: 0.8 g, Total Carbs: 11 g, Protein: 1.1 g.*

Ingredients:

4 bananas

2 Tbsp. cocoa powder

1-2 Tbsp. corn syrup

1 tsp. lemon juice

Instructions:

- Puree all ingredients until smooth.
- Pour mixture onto dehydrator trays and spread to ¼ inch thickness. Dehydrate at 130 degree for 8-10 hours. About half way through, flip leather to the other side.

Cherry Coconut Almond Cookies

These all-natural cookies taste delicious with any combination of dried fruits, nut butter and nuts. Feel free to add sweetened shredded coconut as they contain no other added sugars. Those with peanut allergies can enjoy a delicious cookie made exclusively with almond butter (or cashew butter if preferred).

Nutritional Info (per 1-oz serving): Calories: 151, Sodium: 1 mg, Dietary Fiber: 1.4 g, Total Fat: 12.6 g, Total Carbs: 6.6 g, Protein: 4.6 g.

Ingredients:

   1 cup salted almond butter

   1 cup pitted dates (soaked in water for ½ hour)

   1 cup dried cherries (soaked in water for ½ hour)

   1 cup crushed almonds

   1/8- 1/4 cup water

   1 cup shredded coconut

Instructions:

- In a food processor, pulse the dried fruits. Add almond butter and crushed almonds. Pulse again.

- Add in water slowly until the dough is able to be rolled into balls. Do not allow dough to get too runny. Flatten balls into discs and dip into shredded coconut to adhere to both sides.

- Place on dehydrator sheet and set temperature to 145 degrees. Dehydrate for 3 hours and then flip over to other side for 3 hours.

Chewy Lemony Treats

These fragrant, soft cookies will be requested even by those who are not on a raw food diet. The lemon flavor is refreshing and subtle. For more citrus taste, you can add the zest of one lemon to the batter. The batter tends to be wet so if it is too difficult to handle, add more coconut.

Nutritional Info (per 1-oz serving): Calories: 185, Sodium: 6 mg, Dietary Fiber: 4 g, Total Fat: 16.1 g, Total Carbs: 7 g, Protein: 4.1 g.

Ingredients:

2 cups almonds

2 cups unsweetened coconut flakes

6 Tbsp. lemon juice

1 tsp. vanilla extract

Dash of cinnamon

¼ cup maple syrup

Instructions:

- Place almonds in the food processor and pulse until a flour-like consistency develops.
- Add coconut and process with the ground nuts. Add the lemon juice, (zest if using), vanilla extract, cinnamon and maple syrup.
- Scoop out batter into mini-balls and flatten. Place on dehydrator sheets and dehydrate for 8 hours at 115 degrees for a chewy texture.

Energy Balls

These date balls contain cocoa powder to satisfy chocolate lovers who crave an indulgent snack. While these teats can be eaten raw, the texture is more pleasant after they have been dehydrated.

Nutritional Info (per 1-oz serving): *Calories: 125, Sodium: 35 mg, Dietary Fiber: 1.9 g, Total Fat: 8.9 g, Total Carbs: 11.1 g, Protein: 3.1 g.*

Ingredients:

1 ½ cup raw cashews, soaked

2 cups dates, soaked

½ cup raisins

5 Tbsp. unsweetened cocoa powder

2 Tbsp. maple syrup

½ tsp. vanilla extract

½ tsp. salt

½ cup crushed cashews

½ cup unsweetened coconut flakes

Instructions:

- Remove cashews and dates from soaking water. Place them in a food processor and pulse. Add the raisins, cocoa powder, maple syrup, vanilla extract and salt and blend until it reaches a paste-like consistency.

- Once the mixture feels like a dough, roll into balls. Mix crushed cashews and coconut flakes in a small bowl and roll the balls in the mixture.

- Place balls on dehydrator trays and dry at 135 degrees for 3 hours.

Fruit Sprinkles

Looking for a fun, tasty topping for ice cream sundaes, cupcakes or even cereal? Your kids will love these dehydrated fruit sprinkles and you will appreciate that they are made from healthy, all-natural ingredients.

Nutritional Info (per 1-oz serving): *Calories: 25, Sodium: 0 mg, Dietary Fiber: 0 g, Total Fat: 0 g, Total Carbs: 6.5 g, Protein: 0.1 g.*

Ingredients:

1 cup raspberries or strawberries, hulled

1 Tbsp. sugar

1 Tbsp. orange juice

Zest of 2 lemons

Zest of 2 oranges

Instructions:

- Dice strawberries and raspberries into small pieces.
- Combine with sugar, juice and lemon and orange zest.
- Spread mixture on dehydrator sheets.
- Dehydrate for 6-8 hours at 118 degrees. At this point, fruit should be completely dried.
- Place mixture in a spice grinder and pulse several times until you have sprinkles. Top your favorite treats with fruit sprinkles for added flavor and color.

Goji Berry Leather

Goji berries are wildly popular for their many health benefits. These tiny berries are loaded with Vitamins B and C, beta carotene, iron and phytonutrients that are believed to combat harmful free radicals that damage cells. In this simple fruit leather, goji berries are the star.

Nutritional Info (per 1-oz serving): *Calories: 64, Sodium: 0 mg, Dietary Fiber: 1.6 g, Total Fat: 0.8 g, Total Carbs: 14 g, Protein: 0.5 g.*

Ingredients:

> 1 cup dried goji berries
>
> 2 cups unsweetened applesauce
>
> 2 Tbsp. honey

Instructions:

- Place goji berries in 1 cup of water and let soak until they are rehydrated, about 1 hour.

- Pour berries, soaking water, applesauce and honey into the blender and blend until smooth. Add more water if necessary.

- Spread onto dehydrator sheets and dry at 135 degrees for 6-7 hours.

Honey Banana Walnut Chips

These banana chips have an added crunch with the addition of walnuts. Reminiscent of a slice of banana bread, they will be your go-to snack when you are looking for a sweet dessert.

Nutritional Info (per 1-oz serving): *Calories: 136, Sodium: 1 mg, Dietary Fiber: 2.2 g, Total Fat: 8.2 g, Total Carbs: 15 g, Protein: 3.8 g.*

Ingredients:

4 bananas, peeled and cut into ¼ pieces

¼ cup honey, diluted slightly with water

½ cup crushed walnuts

Instructions:

- Dip banana slices into diluted honey. Sprinkle with crushed walnuts.
- Place bananas on dehydrator trays and dry at 135 degrees for 2 hours. Then set the temperature at 115 degrees and dehydrate for another 6-12 hours.

Nothing But Fruit Bars

Do you want a fruit bar that only has ingredients you can pronounce? These bars are nutrient dense, packed with fiber and so simple to make. Keep in mind that only whole buckwheat grouts will sprout. For best results, choose buckwheat groats in their hulls.

Nutritional Info (per 1-oz serving): *Calories: 98, Sodium: 1 mg, Dietary Fiber: 2.3 g, Total Fat: 1.6 g, Total Carbs: 17.6 g, Protein: 3.6 g.*

Ingredients:

> 2 cups sprouted buckwheat or quinoa
>
> 1 cup dates
>
> 1 cup dried apricots
>
> 1 Tbsp. cinnamon
>
> 1/8 tsp. cardamom
>
> 1 pear or apple, peeled, cored and diced

Instructions:

- Place all ingredients in a blender. Blend until smooth.
- Spread the mixture onto dehydrator trays. Use a spatula to smooth. Dehydrate for 18 hours at 130 degrees.

"PB&G": Peanut Butter, Banana and Graham Cracker Cookie Bars

This version of the classic combination of peanut butter and banana is like a homemade protein bar. Try different types of graham crackers (chocolate, cinnamon etc.) for a unique flavor combination. You should chill these in the refrigerator for at least 8 hours so the mixture sets up adequately.

Nutritional Info (per 1-oz serving): *Calories: 119, Sodium: 89 mg, Dietary Fiber: 2.7 g, Total Fat: 4.8 g, Total Carbs: 16.7 g, Protein: 2.7 g.*

Ingredients:

3 ripe bananas, sliced

½ cup peanut butter

½ cup oats

2 cups graham cracker cookies, crushed

½ cup cacao nibs

Instructions:

- In a bowl, mash the bananas with the peanut butter.
- Mix the oats, graham cracker crumbs, and cacao nibs. Blend with banana and peanut butter mixture.
- Gather into a ball and shape into a rectangle using waxed paper or a buttered spatula.
- Chill for 8 hours or overnight, preferably.
- When you remove chilled dough, slice into ¼ inch slices and dehydrate at 135-145 degrees for 6 hours. The texture of these bars will be more like a cookie and less like a cracker.

Raspberry Banana Fruit Leather

When spreading fruit leather, be sure that the edges are a little thicker, up to ¼ inch, as they dry faster. When it is time to remove them from the dehydrator, check the areas where the mixture is thicker to ensure there is no moisture.

Nutritional Info (per 1-oz serving): *Calories: 36, Sodium: 0 mg, Dietary Fiber: 1.1 g, Total Fat: 0.1 g, Total Carbs: 9 g, Protein: 0.3 g.*

Ingredients:

 1 banana

 1 cup raspberries

 2 Tbsp. raspberry jam

 1 tsp. lemon juice

Instructions:

- Puree banana, raspberries, jam and lemon juice until smooth.
- Spread mixture evenly, about 1/8 inch thick, onto fruit leather sheets.
- Set the temperature to 135 degrees. Dry for 8-10 hours, or until leathery to touch.

Raw Fig Balls

If you like figs, you will love these tasty little snacks. Soak your figs first if they seem particularly dry. If the mixture is not sticking together, add a little water or lemon juice to moisten the dough.

Nutritional Info (per 1-oz serving): *Calories: 141, Sodium: 4 mg, Dietary Fiber: 3 g, Total Fat: 9.7 g, Total Carbs: 12.3 g, Protein: 2.8 g.*

Ingredients:

1 cup raw almonds

10 dried figs

½ cup raisins

½ tsp. almond extract

½ tsp. vanilla extract

¾ cup unsweetened coconut flakes

Instructions:

- Place the almonds in a food processor and pulse until they are ground. Add the figs, raisins and extracts and pulse until well combined.
- Once the mixture is a dough-like consistency, roll into balls. Roll the balls in the coconut flakes.
- Place balls on dehydrator trays and dry at 135 degrees for 4-6 hours.

Spiced Apple Chips

Discover the sweet, slightly spicy and deliciously familiar combination of apples, cinnamon and nutmeg in this delicious snack. In general, when dehydrating fruits like apples and pears, the thinner the slices, the crispier the final product. Thicker slices tend to result in a chewier texture.

Nutritional Info (per 1-oz serving): *Calories: 36, Sodium: 1 mg, Dietary Fiber: 2.7 g, Total Fat: 0.1 g, Total Carbs: 10.3 g, Protein: 0.2 g.*

Ingredients:

  3-4 ripe apples (any variety)

  1 Tbsp. ground cinnamon

  1/8 tsp. either nutmeg, cloves, allspice, ginger or cardamom

  1 Tbsp. sugar

Instructions:

- Slice the apple into thin rounds, between 1/8 – 1/4 inch thick. Peels can be removed or left intact. Remove core and seeds.

- Toss sliced apples with the cinnamon, nutmeg, cloves and sugar.

- Arrange in a single line in your dehydrator and set temperature to 135. Allow apples to dehydrate for 6-8 hours.

Spicy Strawberry Fruit Leather

Have you ever tried fruit leather – for adults? This is it! For an unusual and interesting treat, add heat to sweet fruit. If possible, use an offset spatula to spread the fruit more easily.

Nutritional Info (per 1-oz serving): *Calories:* 67, *Sodium:* 0 *mg, Dietary Fiber:* 0 *g, Total Fat:* 0 *g, Total Carbs:* 17.9 *g, Protein:* 0.1 *g.*

Ingredients:

1 lb strawberries, hulled and chopped

1/3 cup granulated sugar

1 Tbsp. lemon juice

1 jalapeno or serrano pepper, seeds removed

Instructions:

- Puree strawberries, sugar, lemon juice and pepper.
- Pour mixture onto fruit leather sheet of your dehydrator. Spread puree evenly, about 1/8 inch thick, onto drying tray.
- Set the temperature to 140 degrees. Dry for 6-8 hours, or touch center of leather to determine dryness.

Strawberry-Pineapple Fruit Leather

These homemade fruit leathers are so refreshing and delicious; you will never go back to the store-bought variety. Remember to use the fruit leather sheets that come with your dehydrator when preparing fruit leathers.

Nutritional Info (per 1-oz serving): *Calories: 18, Sodium: 0 mg, Dietary Fiber: 0 g, Total Fat: 0.1 g, Total Carbs: 4.5 g, Protein: 0.2 g.*

Ingredients:

2 cups washed, cored and roughly chopped strawberries

1 Tbsp. honey

2 Tbsp. pineapple juice

¾ cup unsweetened applesauce

Nonstick cooking spray

Instructions:

- Puree strawberries with honey and pineapple juice. Add applesauce to mixture and puree again.
- Spray the fruit leather sheet of your dehydrator with cooking spray.
- Pour the pureed fruit mixture onto the tray set in the bottom of your dehydrator.
- Dehydrate at 140 degrees for up to 8 hours. When done, cool for several minutes before rolling into cylinders.

Sweet and Sour Cranberries

You can make everyone's favorite go-to snack right at home! These dried cranberries are perfect for green or grain salads, or as a treat on their own. Substitute these cranberries in any recipe calling for raisins.

Nutritional Info (per 1-oz serving): *Calories: 41, Sodium: 0 mg, Dietary Fiber: 0.6 g, Total Fat: 0 g, Total Carbs: 10.2 g, Protein: 0 g.*

Ingredients:

12 oz. cranberries

¼ cup corn syrup (or sugar)

Zest of one orange and one lime

Instructions:

- Place cranberries in a bowl and pour boiling water over them until the skins crack. Drain.

- Toss the berries with corn syrup or sugar and zests. Place berries on cooking sheet and freeze for 2 hours to promote faster drying.

- Assemble berries on a mesh sheet in the dehydrator and dry at 135 degrees for 12-16 hours or until chewy.

Sweet "Caramel Apples"

Here is a delicious and healthy way to recreate a childhood favorite: caramel apples! They are sweet, crunchy and tart and require just 2 ingredients and a few minutes to prepare.

Nutritional Info (per 1-oz serving): *Calories: 41, Sodium: 45 mg, Dietary Fiber: 0 g, Total Fat: 0 g, Total Carbs: 10.6 g, Protein: 0.2 g.*

Ingredients:

3-4 Granny Smith apples

½ cup store-bought caramel sauce

Instructions:

- Slice the apple into thin rounds, between 1/8-1/4 inch thick. Peels can be removed or left intact. Remove core and seeds.

- Use a pastry brush to spread a small amount of caramel onto each apple round.

- Arrange in a single line in your dehydrator and set temperature to 135 degrees. Allow apples to dehydrate for 10-12 hours.

Sweet Potato- Cinnamon Leather

This simple recipe has only three ingredients and no added sweeteners. Sweet potatoes, which are loaded with Vitamins C and B, potassium, iron and fiber, are considered a superfood. These fruit leathers are a great way to sneak vegetables into your family's diet.

Nutritional Info (per 1-oz serving): *Calories: 33, Sodium: 3 mg, Dietary Fiber: 1.2 g, Total Fat: 0.1 g, Total Carbs: 7.9 g, Protein: 0.4 g.*

Ingredients:

3 medium sweet potatoes

½ tsp. cinnamon

1/8 tsp. ground ginger

Instructions:

- Preheat oven to 400 degrees and place sweet potatoes in a baking dish. Cover and bake 35-45 minutes, or until soft.

- Peel skins and put potatoes in food processor with cinnamon and ginger. Puree until smooth.

- Pour mixture onto dehydrator trays and spread to ¼ inch thickness. Dehydrate at 135 degree for 8-10 hours.

Tangy Dried Mangos

This slightly sweet, mildly tangy fruit treat will be an instant favorite with kids and adults. Freshly squeezed lime juice preserves the mango's color while adding just the right amount of acid.

Nutritional Info (per 1-oz serving): *Calories: 21, Sodium: 1 mg, Dietary Fiber: 0.5 g, Total Fat: 0.1 g, Total Carbs: 5.3 g, Protein: 0.1 g.*

Ingredients:

4-5 ripe mangoes

1 Tbsp. honey

1/4 cup lime juice

Pinch of salt

Instructions:

- Peel and slice mangoes into thin, even strips.
- Dissolve honey in lemon juice. Mix well and add salt.
- Dip mango slices into honey mixture. Shake off excess.
- Arrange in a single line in your dehydrator and set temperature to 135 degrees. Allow mangoes to dehydrate for 8-9 hours.

Tropical Pineapple Crisps

Try dehydrated pineapple with a tasty tropical twist. These crisps have all the taste of a piña colada in a crunchy chip. The addition of coconut flakes provides added texture. A sprinkling of sea salt balances the flavors.

Nutritional Info (per 1-oz serving): *Calories: 51, Sodium: 21 mg, Dietary Fiber: 0.8 g, Total Fat: 2.6 g, Total Carbs: 6.1 g, Protein: 0.7 g.*

Ingredients:

1 ripe pineapple

Coconut oil

½ cup sweetened coconut flakes

Sea salt to taste

Instructions:

- Peel and core the pineapple. Slice into thin, uniform rounds about ½ inch thick.
- Using a pastry brush, spread a thin layer of coconut oil on each pineapple slice. Sprinkle with coconut flakes and a small amount of sea salt.
- Arrange in a single line in your dehydrator and set temperature to 135 degrees. Allow pineapple to dehydrate for 12-16 hours, flipping the slices halfway through for even dryness.

Vanilla-Apricot Slices

The fresh, clean taste of vanilla beans pairs well with many fruits, including apricots. Honey gives these treats just the right hint of sweetness. These apricots are a great twist on the standard dried apricot.

Nutritional Info (per 1-oz serving): Calories: 17, Sodium: 0 mg, Dietary Fiber: 0.5 g, Total Fat: 0.2 g, Total Carbs: 4.1 g, Protein: 0.3 g.

Ingredients:

6-9 medium sized apricots, pitted

1 ½ tsp. honey

4 Tbsp. warm water

Seeds from one vanilla bean, scraped out

Instructions:

- In a bowl, mix honey and vanilla seeds. Add the water and mix well. Combine until vanilla seeds are well separated.
- Slice apricots into thin slices. Place apricot slices onto dehydrator tray and brush on a thin layer of vanilla mixture. It is not necessary for all the vanilla seeds to stick to the fruit.
- Dehydrate for 9-12 hours at 135 degrees.

Watermelon Candy Slices

Some foods do not need many ingredients to bring out their flavors. Watermelon is naturally sweet and refreshing, and tastes perfect when dehydrated on its own without other enhancers. A light sprinkling of fleur de sel, a finishing salt, simply balances the concentrated sweetness of the watermelon.

Nutritional Info (per 1-oz serving): *Calories: 9, Sodium: 0 mg, Dietary Fiber: 0 g, Total Fat: 0 g, Total Carbs: 2.1 g, Protein: 0.2 g.*

Ingredients:

1 watermelon

Fleur de sel

Instructions:

- Cut the watermelon into slices and remove the rinds. Slices should be approximately ¼ inch thick.
- Lay watermelon slices on trays. Sprinkle Fleur de sel on top of the watermelon.
- Place sheets in dehydrator at 135 degrees for 18 hours.

VEGETABLE RECIPES

Brussels Sprouts "Croutons"

If you are on a raw food diet or eating gluten free, these crunchy Brussels sprouts are a great substitute for regular croutons. They are perfect as a topping for salad or simply as a snack. You can omit the nutritional yeast, but it adds a rich, cheesy flavor to the croutons.

Nutritional Info (per 1-oz serving): *Calories: 114, Sodium: 11 mg, Dietary Fiber: 1.5 g, Total Fat: 9.2 g, Total Carbs: 6.7 g, Protein: 3.3 g.*

Ingredients:

16 oz. Brussels sprouts, washed and ends trimmed

½ cup cashews

3 Tbsp. toasted sesame seeds

2 Tbsp. soy sauce

1 tsp. chili powder

1 Tbsp. olive oil

½ tsp. toasted sesame oil

2 Tbsp. lime juice

¼ cup nutritional yeast (optional)

Instructions:

- Place Brussels sprouts in a food processor and pulse them until they are coarsely chopped.
- Add the cashews, sesame seeds, soy sauce, chili powder, olive oil, sesame oil, lime juice and nutritional yeast (if using). Pulse again.
- Pour the Brussels sprout mixture onto a dehydrated sheet and dehydrate for 8-10 hours at 115 degrees.

Cauliflower Poppers

These bite sized treats will soon replace your favorite chip as your late night snack. They are flavored with miso paste, which is a mixture of cooked soybeans, a fermenting agent and water. Purchase the white, rather than red, miso paste for a milder flavor. Miso can be kept refrigerated and used in a variety of food preparations, including soups, sauces, glazes and marinades.

Nutritional Info (per 1-oz serving): *Calories: 22, Sodium: 226 mg, Dietary Fiber: 1.1 g, Total Fat: 0.4 g, Total Carbs: 3.7 g, Protein: 1.3 g.*

Ingredients:

2 heads cauliflower, cut into bite sized pieces

½ cup miso paste

4 Tbsp. water

1 tsp. smoked paprika

1 tsp. garlic powder

1 tsp. onion powder

Instructions:

- Blend all ingredients in a bowl except cauliflower. Add cauliflower and mix well so vegetables are well coated.

- Place cauliflower pieces onto dehydrator sheets and dehydrate at 140 degrees for one hour. Lower the temperature and dehydrate at 110 degrees for another 10 hours or until crispy.

Crunchy Asian Green Beans

These crispy green beans are a fun, delicious snack with an Asian flavor. Green beans should be blanched to prevent an unpleasant color from developing while dehydrating.

Nutritional Info (per 1-oz serving): *Calories: 11, Sodium: 334 mg, Dietary Fiber: 0.9 g, Total Fat: 0 g, Total Carbs: 2.3 g, Protein: 0.8 g.*

Ingredients:

   5 pounds green beans

   1/3 cup melted coconut oil

   1/3 cup soy sauce

   ½ tsp. garlic powder

   ½ tsp. black pepper

Instructions:

- Blanch green beans in boiling water for several minutes. Dry beans.

- Melt coconut oil in microwave. Mix oil, soy sauce and seasonings in a bowl.

- Coast green beans in oil mixture.

- Place green beans onto dehydrator and dry for 8-10 hours at 125 degrees.

Crunchy Kale Chips

These kale chips are not only full of essential vitamins and minerals, they are delicious and highly addictive! The addition of nutritional yeast, which is deactivated yeast in the form of flakes or powder, gives these chips a cheesy, rich flavor without adding excess fat and calories.

Nutritional Info (per 1-oz serving): *Calories: 44, Sodium: 253 mg, Dietary Fiber: 2.8 g, Total Fat: 0.5 g, Total Carbs: 6.5 g, Protein: 5 g.*

Ingredients:

12 oz. bunch curly kale, washed, tough stems removed and leaves roughly torn

2-3 Tbsp. olive oil

1 Tbsp. fresh lemon juice

½ tsp. salt

¼ tsp. pepper

¼ tsp. garlic powder

3 Tbsp. nutritional yeast

Instructions:

- Toss kale, olive oil, lemon juice, salt, pepper and garlic powder in a bowl. Add nutritional yeast.
- Spread kale onto a dehydrator tray.
- Set the temperature to 140 degrees. Dehydrate for 2-4 hours, or until crispy.

Fall Carrot Chips

Try these carrot chips instead of snacking on raw carrots. Coconut oil is a great alternative to other oils. It provides numerous health benefits and a subtle flavor.

Nutritional Info (per 1-oz serving): *Calories: 11, Sodium: 337 mg, Dietary Fiber: 0.7 g, Total Fat: 0 g, Total Carbs: 2.7 g, Protein: 0.2 g.*

Ingredients:

1 pound of carrots, peeled

3 Tbsp. melted coconut oil

¾ tsp. salt

2 tsp. allspice (or combination of cinnamon, allspice or nutmeg)

Instructions:

- Wash, dry and slice carrots into uniform disks.
- Mix together carrots, oil, salt and allspice.
- Place carrots onto dehydrator trays and dry for 6-10 hours at 125 degrees or until crisp.

Herbed Sweet Potato Chips

Making your own potato chips has never been so simple or so delicious. Try these sweet potato chips for an unusual take on store-bought chips. When possible, use a mandolin to achieve the thinnest, most evenly sliced vegetables.

Nutritional Info (per 1-oz serving): *Calories: 35, Sodium: 721 mg, Dietary Fiber: 1.9 g, Total Fat: 0.2 g, Total Carbs: 8.3 g, Protein: 0.6 g.*

Ingredients:

3 medium to large sweet potatoes

4 Tbsp. olive oil

2 Tbsp. fresh lemon juice

2 tsp. dried thyme

1 ½ tsp. salt

¼ tsp. pepper

Instructions:

- Slice sweet potatoes into thin, uniform slices.
- In a bowl combine sweet potato slices, oil, lemon juice, thyme, salt and pepper. Toss until well coated.
- Place slices on dehydrator trays.
- Set the temperature to 140 degrees. Dehydrate for 6-10 hours, or until crisp to touch.

Hot & Spicy Potato Sticks

These potato sticks are great departure from your typical chip. The cumin and peppers create a wonderful flavor, but feel free to substitute any spices you prefer. Potatoes are extremely versatile and stand up well to almost any seasonings.

Nutritional Info (per 1-oz serving): *Calories: 5, Sodium: 1 mg, Dietary Fiber: 0 g, Total Fat: 0.1 g, Total Carbs: 1 g, Protein: 0.1 g.*

Ingredients:

2 large Idaho potatoes, peeled and cut like French fries

3-4 tsp. olive oil

½ tsp. cumin

¼ tsp. black pepper

¼ tsp. cayenne pepper (or more for increased spiciness)

Dash of hot pepper sauce

Salt to taste

Instructions:

- Blanch potatoes in a pot of boiling water for 4-6 minutes.
- Transfer potatoes to a bowl of ice water.
- Combine potatoes, olive oil, cumin, both peppers and hot pepper sauce.
- Lay potatoes onto dehydrator trays.
- Set the dehydrator to 135 degrees and dehydrate for 8-10 hours.

Indian Cauliflower

Cauliflower is an extremely versatile vegetable and holds up well to many flavors. In this recipe, classic Indian spices and a hint of sweetness are combined to create a snack that hits all the right notes. Cauliflower can be blanched first but skipping this will not significantly alter the taste of the final product. The color, however, is preserved better with blanching.

Nutritional Info (per 1-oz serving): *Calories: 20, Sodium: 8 mg, Dietary Fiber: 0.9 g, Total Fat: 0.2 g, Total Carbs: 4.7 g, Protein: 0.6 g.*

Ingredients:

2 heads cauliflower, cut into bite size pieces

¼ cup low sodium soy sauce

1/8 cup honey

1 tsp. curry powder

1 tsp. turmeric

Instructions:

- Blend all ingredients in a bowl except cauliflower. Whisk to ensure honey is incorporated. Add cauliflower and mix well so vegetables are well coated.

- Place cauliflower pieces onto dehydrator sheets and dehydrate at 140 degrees for one hour. Lower the temperature and dehydrate at 110 degrees for another 10 hours or until crispy.

Lemon Pepper Yellow Squash Rounds

These yellow squash chips are both spicy and acidic, and a great use for lemon pepper seasoning. If chips seem greasy after dehydrating, blot lightly with paper towel.

Nutritional Info (per 1-oz serving): *Calories: 5, Sodium: 3 mg, Dietary Fiber: 0 g, Total Fat: 0.1 g, Total Carbs: 0.9 g, Protein: 0.3 g.*

Ingredients:

2 large yellow squash, cut into 1/8" thick rounds

3-4 tsp. olive oil

1 Tbsp. lemon juice

½ tsp. lemon pepper seasoning

Salt to taste

Instructions:

- Toss squash slices with olive oil until well coated. Add lemon juice, lemon pepper seasoning and salt and combine all ingredients thoroughly.
- Spread squash onto dehydrator trays.
- Set the dehydrator to 135 degrees and dehydrate for 10-12 hours. Halfway through, flip each chip over to prevent sticking.

Marinated Eggplant

If you are a vegetarian, these dehydrated eggplant sticks will give you the texture and flavor of a jerky without the meat. Refrigerating the marinated eggplant allows the flavors to set.

Nutritional Info (per 1-oz serving): *Calories: 17, Sodium: 7 mg, Dietary Fiber: 0.8 g, Total Fat: 0.1 g, Total Carbs: 4.3 g, Protein: 0.2 g.*

Ingredients:

1 eggplant, peeled or unpeeled

¼ cup olive oil

4 Tbsp. balsamic vinegar

2 Tbsp. maple syrup

½ tsp. sriracha sauce

Salt and pepper to taste

Instructions:

- Slice eggplant into long, uniform strips.
- Combine oil, vinegar, maple syrup and srircaha sauce with eggplant in a bowl. Sprinkle on salt and pepper to taste. Refrigerate for a minimum of 2 hours.
- Place eggplant on dehydrator trays and dehydrate for 12-18 hours at 115 degrees.

Mediterranean Style "Sun-Dried" Tomatoes

These tomatoes are a delicious addition to any salad, pasta or grain, but are just as delicious eaten on their own. Use a variety of dried herbs for a unique Italian flavor.

Nutritional Info (per 1-oz serving): *Calories: 5, Sodium: 325 mg, Dietary Fiber: 0 g, Total Fat: 0.1 g, Total Carbs: 1.1 g, Protein: 0.2 g.*

Ingredients:

4 large firm, ripe tomatoes

1 ½ tsp. mixed dried herbs, such as oregano, thyme and basil

½ tsp. sea salt

Instructions:

- Wash tomatoes and cut off tops. Tomatoes do not need to peeled and seeded. Slice tomatoes into ¼ inch thick slices.
- Sprinkle tomatoes with herbs and salt and place on dehydrator trays.
- Set the dehydrator to 145 degrees and dehydrate for 8-10 hours, or until leathery.

Moroccan Carrot Crunch

These carrot chips have all the flavor and spice of Moroccan carrot salad. Enjoy them as an accompaniment to your favorite dip, such as humus and white bean dip.

Nutritional Info (per 1-oz serving): *Calories: 26, Sodium: 262 mg, Dietary Fiber: 0.7 g, Total Fat: 0.3 g, Total Carbs: 6 g, Protein: 0.5 g.*

Ingredients:

> 1 pound of carrots, peeled
>
> 4 Tbsp. olive oil
>
> 1 Tbsp. honey
>
> 1/8 tsp. cayenne pepper
>
> 2 tsp. cumin
>
> 1 tsp. dried parsley flakes
>
> ½ tsp. salt

Instructions:

- Wash, dry and thinly slice carrots.
- Mix together oil, honey, and seasonings.
- Place carrots onto dehydrator trays. Using a pastry brush, dab the mixture onto the carrot rounds.
- Dehydrate for 6-10 hours at 125 degrees or until crisp.

Parmesan Cucumber Chips

Cucumbers are a great alternative to zucchini to create crunchy, healthy chips. These cucumber chips get their savory cheesy flavor from a generous sprinkling of parmesan cheese. If you do not eat dairy, substitute nutritional yeast to achieve a similar flavor.

Nutritional Info (per 1-oz serving): *Calories: 39, Sodium: 220 mg, Dietary Fiber: 0 g, Total Fat: 2.4 g, Total Carbs: 1.1 g, Protein: 3.7 g.*

Ingredients:

5 cups cucumber slices, thinly sliced with a mandolin

2 Tbsp. olive oil

½ tsp. salt

¼ tsp. black pepper

½ tsp. dried parsley flakes

½ cup freshly grated parmesan cheese

Instructions:

- Mix the salt, pepper, parsley flakes and parmesan cheese in a bowl. Toss sliced cucumbers with olive oil and combine with seasoning and cheese mixture. Coat the slices well.
- Place slices on dehydrator sheets and dehydrate for 8-10 hours at 135 degrees.

Ranch Brussels Sprout Skins

When you roast Brussels sprouts in the oven, the best part is always the crispy almost blackened outer skins that fall off the sprout. That is the inspiration for this recipe. With the addition of a ranch inspired spice combination, these crispy sprouts will become a new family favorite.

Nutritional Info (per 1-oz serving): *Calories: 16, Sodium: 104 mg, Dietary Fiber: 0.8 g, Total Fat: 0.2 g, Total Carbs: 3 g, Protein: 1.1 g.*

Ingredients:

4 cups Brussels sprouts, coarsely chopped, tough centers discarded

1 cup buttermilk

1 tsp. mustard

3 Tbsp. oil

½ tsp. salt

1 tsp. onion powder

1 tsp. minced garlic flakes

1 tsp. dried dill

1 tsp. dried parsley

1 tsp. celery salt

Instructions:

- Place sliced Brussels sprouts in a bowl. Blend the seasonings in another small bowl.
- Whisk together buttermilk, mustard and oil. Pour over Brussels sprouts.

- Spray dehydrator tray with nonstick spray and place Brussels sprouts on tray. Sprinkle with seasonings. Set the dehydrator to 110 degrees and dehydrate for 8-10 hours.

Root Vegetable Medley

These days you will find dozens of root vegetable chips in the snack aisle of your grocery store. The recipe below combines your favorite root vegetables with simple seasonings to create a colorful, crunchy, salty snack. Be sure to scrub these vegetables thoroughly as they tend to have a fair amount of dirt on them. Root vegetables cook at different rates so separate them on different dehydrator trays.

Nutritional Info (per 1-oz serving): *Calories: 48, Sodium: 737 mg, Dietary Fiber: 2.1 g, Total Fat: 0.2 g, Total Carbs: 11 g, Protein: 1.3 g.*

Ingredients:

2 medium beets

1 sweet potato

2 medium parsnips

1 medium celery root

3 Tbsp. olive oil

1 ½ tsp. salt

1 tsp. garlic powder

½ tsp. oregano

Pinch of black pepper

Instructions:

- Wash, peel and slice vegetables as thinly as possible, preferably with a mandolin.
- Place vegetables in a bowl. Mix olive oil with seasonings and pour over vegetables. Toss to coat.
- Lay vegetables on trays using different trays for different vegetables. Dehydrate at 105 degrees for at least 8 hours.

Salt & Pepper Vinegar Zucchini Chips

What do you do with the bounty of leftover zucchini from your garden every summer? Make zucchini chips! These taste very similar to the salt & vinegar potato chips from the bag, but are fresher and healthier.

Nutritional Info (per 1-oz serving): *Calories: 7, Sodium: 338 mg, Dietary Fiber: 0 g, Total Fat: 0 g, Total Carbs: 1.8 g, Protein: 0.2 g.*

Ingredients:

2 large green zucchini, cut into 1/8" thick rounds

3-4 tsp. olive oil

1 Tbsp. + 1 tsp. apple cider vinegar

Salt & pepper to taste

Instructions:

- Toss zucchini slices with olive oil until well coated. Add vinegar, salt and pepper and combine.
- Spread zucchini onto a dehydrator tray.
- Set the dehydrator to 135 degrees and dehydrate for 10-12 hours. Halfway through, flip each chip over to prevent sticking.

Salt and Vinegar Cucumber Chips

Discover the salty, pungent flavor of vinegar chips in a cucumber! These chips are a great way to use all the cucumbers your garden produces during the summer.

Nutritional Info (per 1-oz serving): *Calories: 6, Sodium: 0 mg, Dietary Fiber: 0.6 g, Total Fat: 0 g, Total Carbs: 1.2 g, Protein: 0.3 g.*

Ingredients:

2 large cucumbers, peeled and sliced thins

2 tsp. apple cider vinegar

1 tsp. fresh lemon juice

½ tsp. kosher salt

½ tsp. sugar

Instructions:

- In a bowl, whisk together vinegar, lemon juice, salt and sugar. Add cucumbers and toss in dressing.

- Place cucumber slices on dehydrator tray and dehydrate for 4-6 hours at 135 degrees.

Smoked Collard Green Chips

Collard greens are the "new" kale. These collard green chips have a smoky taste and provide many of the same nutritional benefits as kale.

Nutritional Info (per 1-oz serving): *Calories: 16, Sodium: 262 mg, Dietary Fiber: 0.7 g, Total Fat: 0.1 g, Total Carbs: 3.4 g, Protein: 0.9 g.*

Ingredients:

1 bunch collard greens, washed and leaves roughly torn

3 Tbsp. olive oil

½ tsp. smoked paprika

½ tsp. sea salt

¼ tsp. pepper

Instructions:

- Toss collard greens, olive oil and spices in a bowl.
- Place collard greens onto a dehydrator tray.
- Set the temperature to 140 degrees. Dehydrate for 2-4 hours, or until crispy.

Smoky Sweet Potato Chips

A hint of smoked paprika gives these sweet potatoes a savory barbecue flavor. Remember to blanch potatoes first to maintain color and flavor.

Nutritional Info (per 1-oz serving): Calories: 37, Sodium: 3 mg, Dietary Fiber: 1.8 g, Total Fat: 0.3 g, Total Carbs: 8.5 g, Protein: 0.7 g.

Ingredients:

3 large sweet potatoes, washed and sliced into very thin slices

2 tsp. olive oil

1 ½ tsp. smoked paprika

Sea salt to taste

Instructions:

- Blanch potatoes in a pot of boiling water for 4-6 minutes.
- Transfer potatoes to a bowl of ice water.
- Combine sliced potatoes, olive oil, smoked paprika and salt.
- Lay potatoes onto dehydrator trays.
- Set the dehydrator to 135 degrees and dehydrate for 8-10 hours, or until crispy.

Spinach Balls

Spinach balls make a great snack or appetizer for a party with their vibrant green color and crunchy exterior. Cashews are used here and in other recipes as the base for the marinade. Nutmeg and spinach are naturally complementary flavors.

Nutritional Info (per 1-oz serving): *Calories: 137, Sodium: 7 mg, Dietary Fiber: 0.9 g, Total Fat: 10.5 g, Total Carbs: 9.2 g, Protein: 3.7 g.*

Ingredients:

3 cups cashews

3 cups blanched spinach

4 Tbsp. olive oil

¼ cup dehydrated onion flakes

3 cloves of garlic

¼ tsp. nutmeg

Pinch of cayenne pepper

Instructions:

- Process the cashews until they are finely ground. Add all the remaining ingredients and pulse several times until well combined and paste-like in consistency.

- Pour mixture into a bowl and form into small, bite-size balls.

- Place spinach balls on dehydrator sheets and dehydrate at 120 degrees for 5 hours.

Sour Cream and Onion Potato Chips

You can make one of your favorite flavored chips without the added fat and preservatives! This recipe can be made with either a blender or an immersion blender. Try to spread the mixture as thinly as possible on the dehydrator trays to ensure a "chip-like" consistency.

Nutritional Info (per 1-oz serving): *Calories: 40, Sodium: 505 mg, Dietary Fiber: 0.6 g, Total Fat: 2.2 g, Total Carbs: 4.7 g, Protein: 0.9 g.*

Ingredients:

2 large russet potatoes, washed, peeled and sliced into chunks

½ cup sour cream

1 ½ cups water

1 Tbsp. onion powder

1 Tbsp. minced onion

1 Tbsp. dried parsley

1 ½ tsp. salt

½ tsp. black pepper

Instructions:

- Cook potatoes in a pot of boiling water until soft.
- Drain potatoes when done and place in a bowl with the remaining ingredients.
- Use an immersion blender to create a soft paste.
- Use a spatula to smooth the paste onto the dehydrator sheets in a fairly thin layer.
- Set the dehydrator to 145 degrees. Place trays in dehydrator for 4-6 hours. Flip and return to the dehydrator for several hours, for a total of 9-10 hours.

- Once cooled, break into smaller pieces.

Southwestern Style Cauliflower Popcorn

Ditch the buttery popcorn for this crunchy, spicy treat. Dehydrated cauliflower is a great stand-in for corn, both in appearance and texture. Once the cauliflower is very crispy, you might not even recognize that it is actually cauliflower! Vary the spices you use to customize the heat level.

Nutritional Info (per 1-oz serving): *Calories: 17, Sodium: 212 mg, Dietary Fiber: 1.6 g, Total Fat: 0.5 g, Total Carbs: 3.1 g, Protein: 1 g.*

Ingredients:

1 head cauliflower, cut into bite sized pieces

1 tsp. paprika

1 tsp. oregano

1 tsp. coriander

1 tsp. cumin

¼ tsp. onion powder

¼ tsp. garlic powder

1/8 – ¼ tsp. cayenne pepper

½ tsp. salt

3 Tbsp. olive oil

Instructions:

- Blend all the seasonings and olive oil in a bowl. Add cauliflower and combine to coat all the florets.

- Place cauliflower pieces onto dehydrator sheets and dehydrate at 140 degrees for one hour. Lower the temperature and dehydrate at 110 degrees for another 10 hours or until crispy.

Sweet Kale Chips

These chips are an interesting twist on your standard kale chip. Instead of a savory chip, they have a hint of sweetness and acidity. Without the addition of oil, these chips retain a crispy texture.

Nutritional Info (per 1-oz serving): *Calories: 108, Sodium: 5 mg, Dietary Fiber: 1.3 g, Total Fat: 7.9 g, Total Carbs: 9.4 g, Protein: 1.9 g.*

Ingredients:

1 bunch curly kale, washed, tough stems removed and leaves roughly torn

½ cup pine nuts

1/8-1/4 cup white sugar

½ Tbsp. cinnamon

1/3 cup water

1/8 cup apple cider vinegar

Instructions:

- Place pine nuts, sugar and cinnamon in a food processor.
- Blend water and vinegar and add slowly to food processor.
- Pour mixture over kale and mix until coated.
- Place on dehydrating trays for 2-4 hours at 140 degrees.

Sweet and Savory Beet Rounds

Beets are delicious when dried and crunchy. They are naturally flavorful and the addition of rosemary is a great complement to their natural sweetness.

Nutritional Info (per 1-oz serving): *Calories: 21, Sodium: 539 mg, Dietary Fiber: 1.9 g, Total Fat: 0.5 g, Total Carbs: 4.6 g, Protein: 0.6 g.*

Ingredients:

4 large beets, washed

2 Tbsp. olive oil

1 tsp. fresh rosemary, finely chopped

½ tsp. sea salt

¼ tsp. pepper

Instructions:

- Cut tops of beets. Slice beets about 1/8-1/4 inch wide. Use a mandolin if possible.
- Toss beets, olive oil, rosemary, salt and pepper in a bowl until evenly coated.
- Set the dehydrator to 145 degrees. Place trays in dehydrator for 10-12 hours.

Tex-Mex Green Beans

In a variation on crispy green beans, south-of-the-border flavors are added for a spicy and savory snack. You can increase or decrease the various spices to suit your taste. Use the freshest produce possible for best results.

Nutritional Info (per 1-oz serving): *Calories: 12, Sodium: 7 mg, Dietary Fiber: 1.1 g, Total Fat: 0.2 g, Total Carbs: 2.4 g, Protein: 0.6 g.*

Ingredients:

5 pounds green beans

1/3 cup melted coconut oil

1 tsp. chili powder

1 tsp. cumin

½ tsp. each paprika, onion powder, garlic powder, salt and pepper

Instructions:

- Blanch green beans in boiling water for several minutes. Dry beans.

- Melt coconut oil in microwave. Mix oil and seasonings in a bowl.

- Coast green beans in oil mixture.

- Place green beans onto dehydrator and dry for 8-10 hours at 125 degrees.

Vegan Broccoli Crisps

If you want to get your kids to eat their broccoli, look no further than these salty, savory broccoli crisps. Your kids won't even know that the cheese has been substituted for nutritional yeast. This recipe is ideal for vegans.

Nutritional Info (per 1-oz serving): *Calories: 104, Sodium: 8 mg, Dietary Fiber: 2.3 g, Total Fat: 6.8 g, Total Carbs: 8 g, Protein: 5.1 g.*

Ingredients:

2 heads broccoli, washed and cut into bite size florets

½ cup cashews, soaked for at least 1 hour and drained

4 Tbsp. nutritional yeast

1 tsp. curry powder

½ tsp. red pepper flakes

Instructions:

- Blend the cashews, nutritional yeast and spices in a food processor. Add water to achieve a smooth texture. Nuts should be fully blended.

- Pour dressing into a bowl and add broccoli. Coat the florets evenly.

- Place florets onto dehydrator sheets and dehydrate at 110 degrees for 18 hours.

MEAT RECIPES

Asian Jerky

This jerky has a touch of ginger and sesame for an Asian flavor. As an additional safety measure, heat meat strips in oven for 10 minutes at 275 degrees after dehydrating is complete.

Nutritional Info (per 1-oz serving): *Calories: 50, Sodium: 66 mg, Dietary Fiber: 0 g, Total Fat: 1.3 g, Total Carbs: 3.1 g, Protein: 6.1 g.*

Ingredients:

1 pound sliced lean beef

4 Tbsp. soy sauce

4 Tbsp. Worcestershire sauce

1 tsp. ground ginger

½ tsp. pepper

3 cloves garlic

1 tsp. toasted sesame oil

1 tsp. honey

Instructions:

- Cut strips into ¼ inch thick slices.
- Blend ingredients and coat meat strips in sauce.
- Cover and refrigerate overnight.
- Place meat slices on dehydrator trays and dry at 145-155 degrees for 6-10 hours.

BBQ Jerky Strips

Ground beef is extremely affordable, making it a great choice for dehydrating a large batch of beef jerky. This recipe calls for barbecue sauce. While any type works well, the hickory smoke complements this recipe. Jerky cannons are extremely useful for shaping ground meats. They are generally sold as a separate accessory by the major dehydrator brands.

Nutritional Info (per 1-oz serving): *Calories: 54, Sodium: 329 mg, Dietary Fiber: 0 g, Total Fat: 1.2 g, Total Carbs: 4.6 g, Protein: 5.8 g.*

Ingredients:

2 ½ pounds lean ground beef

2 tsp. salt

½ tsp. garlic powder

½ tsp. onion powder

1 ½ Tbsp. brown sugar

¼ cup Worcestershire sauce

½ cup barbecue sauce, slightly diluted with water

Instructions:

- Mix ground beef with dry ingredients until incorporated.
- Combine liquids and coat beef strips with sauce.
- Press strips into jerky gun. Squeeze onto dehydrator trays and dry at 145-155 degrees for 6-12 hours.

Bold Beef Jerky

The jerky in this recipe has intense flavors and bold ingredients. Only use dehydrators with temperature controls when dehydrating meat to make sure that meat is dehydrated to the proper temperature.

Nutritional Info (per 1-oz serving): *Calories: 51, Sodium: 27 mg, Dietary Fiber: 0 g, Total Fat: 1.7 g, Total Carbs: 0 g, Protein: 8.3 g.*

Ingredients:

2 pounds sliced lean meat

¼ cup soy sauce

1 Tbsp. Worcestershire sauce

1 tsp. hot sauce

¼ tsp. pepper

¼ tsp. garlic powder

¼ tsp. onion powder

¼ tsp. paprika

1 tsp. liquid smoke

Instructions:

- Cut strips into ¼ inch thick slices.
- Mix all ingredients and coat meat strips.
- Cover and refrigerate overnight.
- Place meat slices on dehydrator trays and dry at 145-155 degrees for 6-10 hours.

Boozy Jerky

This jerky gets its flavor from a dark Belgian ale. Be sure to choose a high quality dark, sweet beer rather than a light variety. Beer is traditionally used as a meat marinade to flavor and tenderize the beef.

Nutritional Info (per 1-oz serving): *Calories: 60, Sodium: 76 mg, Dietary Fiber: 0 g, Total Fat: 1.6 g, Total Carbs: 3.5 g, Protein: 7.6 g.*

Ingredients:

2 pounds lean steak, trimmed and frozen up to 2 hours prior to slicing

16 ounces dark Belgian beer

2 Tbsp. teriyaki sauce

¼ cup soy sauce

2 Tbsp. dark brown sugar

½ tsp. seasoned salt

2 cloves of garlic, minced

½ tsp. cayenne pepper

Instructions:

- Mix the marinade ingredients in a large bowl. Place meat in a Ziplock bag and pour marinade over meat.
- Keep meat in refrigerator overnight.
- Remove from refrigerator and let meat come to room temperature.
- Lay meat on dehydrator sheets in a single layer.
- Dehydrate at 160 degrees for 6-8 hours.

Garlicky Beef Jerky

Coke is typically used in meat marinades to tenderize the meat, but it can also be used as a sugar-base in a marinade. This serves as a nice balance to the jerky's natural salty and savory flavor.

Nutritional Info (per 1-oz serving): *Calories: 52, Sodium: 60 mg, Dietary Fiber: 0 g, Total Fat: 1.6 g, Total Carbs: 1.1 g, Protein: 7.7 g.*

Ingredients:

2 pounds thinly sliced beef

1 can of coke

7 cloves crushed garlic

½ cup soy sauce

3 Tbsp. Worcestershire sauce

2 Tbsp. ketchup

2 tsp. red hot sauce

1 tsp. fresh lime juice

Instructions:

- Combine the marinade ingredients in a large bowl. Place meat in a Ziplock bag and pour marinade over meat.
- Marinate meat in refrigerator for 4-8 hours.
- Lay meat on dehydrator sheets in a single layer.
- Dehydrate at 155 degrees for 6-8 hours.

Marinated Jerky

This lightly seasoned jerky is a great introduction to dehydrated meats. This recipe calls for the meat to be brined, which means the meat is soaked in a salt/sugar solution to tenderize it prior to cooking or dehydrating. It is preferable to freeze the meat before slicing.

Nutritional Info (per 1-oz serving): *Calories: 54, Sodium: 1,842 mg, Dietary Fiber: 0 g, Total Fat: 1.2 g, Total Carbs: 5 g, Protein: 5.8 g.*

Ingredients:

2 pounds sliced lean meat

½ gallon water

¼ cup plus 1 Tbsp. salt

¼ cup sugar

2 Tbsp. liquid smoke

½ tsp. black pepper

½ tsp. smoked paprika

Instructions:

- Cut strips into ¼ inch thick slices. Prepare the brine by mixing all the ingredients.
- Soak meat strips in the brine overnight.
- Pour off brine. Rinse and pat meat dry.
- Place meat slices on dehydrator trays and dry at 145-155 degrees for 6-10 hours.

Orange Flavored Beef Jerky

If you are craving Chinese takeout, this flavorful jerky has all the taste of a Chinese classic and can stay fresh for a month in the refrigerator. The jerky can also be frozen for up to several months.

Nutritional Info (per 1-oz serving): *Calories: 61, Sodium: 16 mg, Dietary Fiber: 0 g, Total Fat: 1.6 g, Total Carbs: 4.3 g, Protein: 7.3 g.*

Ingredients:

   3 pounds lean beef, trimmed of all fat and sliced into strips 1/8 inches -3/8 inches thick

   3 oranges, (2 peeled and juiced, and 1 zested)

   3 Tbsp. soy sauce

   3 Tbsp. rice vinegar

   2 Tbsp. sugar

   3 Tbsp. sesame oil

   1 ½ Tbsp. toasted sesame oil

   1 tsp. Asian chili-garlic paste

   2 Tbsp. fresh ginger, grated

Instructions:

- Place all the ingredients, except for the beef, into a blender and process until smooth.
- Pour marinade over meat and mix.
- Keep marinated meat in refrigerator overnight.
- Remove from refrigerator and let meat come to room temperature.
- Lay meat on dehydrator sheets in a single layer.

- Dehydrate at 145-160 degrees for 6-10 hours.

Pastrami Jerky

Pastrami jerky takes the great flavor of cured meat and captures it in a jerky-style snack. Whole spices give it the taste and appearance of deli-style pastrami.

Nutritional Info (per 1-oz serving): *Calories: 56, Sodium: 50 mg, Dietary Fiber: 0 g, Total Fat: 1.4 g, Total Carbs: 4.2 g, Protein: 6.1 g.*

Ingredients:

3 pounds lean beef, such as flank

½ cup soy sauce

¼ cup brown sugar

½ cup Worcestershire sauce

1 Tbsp. lemon juice

½ tsp. cayenne pepper

2 Tbsp. coarse pepper seeds

2 Tbsp. coriander seeds

1 Tbsp. mustard seeds

Instructions:

- Cut each slice of beef into ¼ inch thick strips.
- Combine all ingredients except seeds. Pour ingredients over sliced meat and refrigerate overnight.
- Remove from refrigerator and let meat come to room temperature.
- Lay meat on dehydrator sheets and sprinkle with seeds.
- Dehydrate at 145-155 degrees for 6-10 hours.

Salmon Jerky

Jerky is not just for beef and turkey. Fish jerky is a great way to use leftover fish and create a nutritious snack that can be stored for future use. If possible, purchase wild salmon, which is free of antibiotics and hormones.

Nutritional Info (per 1-oz serving): *Calories: 36, Sodium: 166 mg, Dietary Fiber: 0 g, Total Fat: 1.4 g, Total Carbs: 1.3 g, Protein: 4.7 g.*

Ingredients:

1 ½ pounds salmon, bones removed

¼ cup soy sauce

¼ cup teriyaki sauce

1 Tbsp. Dijon mustard

1 Tbsp. maple syrup

1 freshly squeezed lime

½ tsp. black pepper

Ingredients:

- Freeze salmon for 45 minutes to 1 hour prior to slicing.
- Place remaining ingredients in a bowl and whisk together.
- Slice salmon into thin strips and add them to the liquid. Marinate for 3 hours.
- Remove salmon strips, pat dry and place on dehydrator sheets.
- Dehydrate for 10-12 hours at 155 degrees.

"Smoked" Turkey

This recipe for turkey jerky is simple but has a deep flavor that comes from the smoke-infused ingredients. Because turkey is not naturally very flavorful, it goes well with many different, bold flavor combinations.

Nutritional Info (per 1-oz serving): *Calories: 72, Sodium: 14 mg, Dietary Fiber: 1.2 g, Total Fat: 1.5 g, Total Carbs: 10 g, Protein: 5.6 g.*

Ingredients:

> 1 pound, skinless, boneless turkey
>
> ¼ cup brown sugar
>
> ¾ cup soy sauce
>
> 2 Tbsp. liquid smoke
>
> 1 Tbsp. smoked paprika
>
> ½ Tbsp. paprika

Instructions:

- Slice turkey into ¼ inch thick strips.
- Combine all ingredients and pour over turkey strips. Cover turkey and refrigerate 4-6 hours.
- Place turkey slices on dehydrator trays and dry at 155 degrees for 12-16 hours. Rotate trays occasionally to ensure consistent dehydration.

Smokey Mexican Jerky

The chipotles in this Mexican Jerky impart a distinct smoky flavor. You can find canned Chipotle peppers in the Latin aisle of most supermarkets. Remember to scrape the seeds from the peppers or the heat will overpower the jerky.

Nutritional Info (per 1-oz serving): *Calories: 59, Sodium: 24 mg, Dietary Fiber: 0.6 g, Total Fat: 1.7 g, Total Carbs: 2.7 g, Protein: 8.2 g.*

Ingredients:

2 pounds beef top round or bottom round, fat trimmed, sliced into ¼ inch thick slices

½ cup soy sauce

1 cup fresh lime juice

1-2 canned chipotle peppers in adobo sauce

1 tsp. chili powder

1 cup Mexican beer

Instructions:

- Place all the ingredients, except for the beef, into a blender and process until smooth.
- Pour marinade over meat and refrigerate for 6-8 hours.
- Remove from refrigerator and place meat on dehydrator sheets in a single layer.
- Dehydrate at 145-160 degrees for 6-10 hours.

Spiced "Hamburger" Jerky

Use the leanest possible ground beef to create a beef jerky product that dehydrates well. When working with a jerky gun, make sure to keep the meat very cold.

Nutritional Info (per 1-oz serving): *Calories: 52, Sodium: 319 mg, Dietary Fiber: 0 g, Total Fat: 1.3 g, Total Carbs: 3.5 g, Protein: 6.2 g.*

Ingredients:

2 ½ pounds lean ground beef

1 tsp. Adobo seasoning

2 tsp. salt

½ tsp. garlic powder

½ tsp. onion powder

1 Tbsp. meat tenderizer

½ tsp. cayenne pepper

¼ cup tomato sauce

1 ½ Tbsp. brown sugar

¼ cup Worcestershire sauce

¼ cup liquid smoke

Instructions:

- Mix ground beef with dry ingredients until seasonings are well distributed.
- Combine liquids and coat beef strips with sauce.

  Press strips into jerky gun. Squeeze onto dehydrator trays and dry at 145-155 degrees for 6-12 hours.

Spiced Turkey Jerky

If you are looking for a delicious jerky preparation but want a leaner protein, try this turkey jerky recipe. Be sure to trim any remaining fat from turkey prior to dehydrating.

Nutritional Info (per 1-oz serving): *Calories: 62, Sodium: 17 mg, Dietary Fiber: 0 g, Total Fat: 1.4 g, Total Carbs: 5.1 g, Protein: 6.9 g.*

Ingredients:

2 pounds skinless, boneless turkey

¾ cup soy sauce

3 Tbsp. brown sugar

2 tsp. chopped garlic

2 tsp. red chili flakes

Instructions:

- Freeze turkey prior to slicing. Cut into ¼ inch thick strips.
- Combine all ingredients and dip turkey strips into mixture.
- Cover turkey strips and refrigerate overnight.
- Place turkey slices on dehydrator trays and dry at 155 degrees for 8-10 hours.

Spicy Harissa Flavored Jerky

The chili powder and other seasonings in this recipe come together to create a "harissa" flavor. This dry preparation produces a less oily jerky which tends to stay fresh for a longer time. When dehydrating meats, always read machine instructions for time and temperature recommendations – meats are typically dehydrated for anywhere from 4 to 12 hours.

Nutritional Info (per 1-oz serving): *Calories: 56, Sodium: 692 mg, Dietary Fiber: 0.9 g, Total Fat: 1.8 g, Total Carbs: 3.5 g, Protein: 6.9 g.*

Ingredients:

3 pounds lean beef, such as bottom round or eye of round

2 Tbsp. salt

1 Tbsp. brown sugar

1 Tbsp. chili powder

1 Tbsp. smoked paprika

1 Tbsp. cumin

1 Tbsp. coriander

1 Tbsp. garlic powder

1 Tbsp. onion powder

¼ tsp. cayenne pepper

Instructions:

- Cut each slice of beef into ¼ inch thick strips.
- Combine ingredients and pour into Ziplock bag. Add the meat strips and and refrigerate overnight.
- Remove from refrigerator and let meat come to room temperature.

- Lay meat on dehydrator sheets and dehydrate at 145-155 degrees for 6-10 hours.

Sweet and Spicy Venison or Beef Jerky

Be sure to freeze venison before dehydrating to kill any harmful bacteria. The pineapple juice in this recipe adds a tart sweetness to complement the heat from the sriracha sauce.

Nutritional Info (per 1-oz serving): *Calories: 53, Sodium: 22 mg, Dietary Fiber: 1.1 g, Total Fat: 0.4 g, Total Carbs: 9.5 g, Protein: 3.5 g.*

Ingredients:

2 pounds venison or beef

½ cup brown sugar

¼ cup pineapple juice

1 Tbsp. black pepper

1 Tbsp. lemon juice

1 Tbsp. minced garlic

1 Tbsp. paprika

¼ cup Worcestershire sauce

½ cup soy sauce

1 tsp. sriracha sauce

Instructions:

- Cut pre-frozen venison or beef into ¼ inch thick slices.
- Mix all ingredients and coat strips in the sauce.
- Cover and refrigerate overnight.
- Place beef or venison slices on dehydrator trays and dry at 145-155 degrees about 6-10 hours.

Thai Sweet Chili Jerky

Thai sweet chili sauce is a combination of chili peppers, vinegar, sugar, salt and starch. It is a popular Asian condiment, but also works well as a marinade for beef and chicken. The sugar in the sauce balances the heat from the peppers and complements the umami flavor of the jerky.

Nutritional Info (per 1-oz serving): *Calories: 59, Sodium: 131 mg, Dietary Fiber: 0.6 g, Total Fat: 1.1 g, Total Carbs: 5 g, Protein: 5.6 g.*

Ingredients:

2 pounds beef top or bottom round, trimmed, cut into ¼ inch slices

3 Tbsp. soy sauce

1 Tbsp. Worcestershire sauce

1 Tbsp. teriyaki sauce

½ cup water

1 cup sweet chili sauce

1 tsp. ground ginger

Instructions:

- Combine the marinade ingredients in a large bowl. Place meat in a Ziplock bag and pour marinade over meat.
- Marinate meat in refrigerator overnight.
- Place meat on dehydrator sheets in a single layer.
- Dehydrate at 155 degrees for 6-8 hours.

Teriyaki Jerky

Teriyaki is a versatile marinade ingredient for any meat preparation. During the dehydration process, when using this recipe or any jerky recipe, pat jerky with paper towels to removed accumulated oils.

Nutritional Info (per 1-oz serving): *Calories: 48, Sodium: 276 mg, Dietary Fiber: 0 g, Total Fat: 1 g, Total Carbs: 5 g, Protein: 4.7 g.*

Ingredients:

2 ½ pounds sliced lean beef

1 cup teriyaki sauce

1 cup Worcestershire sauce

½ cup soy sauce

2 tsp. onion powder

2 tsp. garlic powder

1 tsp. paprika

1 tsp. ground ginger

1 Tbsp. red pepper flakes

3 Tbsp. honey

1 tsp. lemon juice

Instructions:

- Cut strips into ¼ inch thick slices.
- Mix ingredients together and marinate meat in sauce mixture.
- Cover and refrigerate overnight.
- Place meat slices on dehydrator trays and dry at 145-155 degrees for 6-10 hours.

GRAINS, NUTS AND SEEDS RECIPES

Apple and Nut "Raw" Cereal

If you are looking for ideas for a "raw" breakfast, then look no further! This apple and nut cereal has a more interesting texture and flavor than a smoothie and far fewer calories and trans-fats than a store-bought cereal. This cereal contains wheat berries, which are the entire wheat kernel. They have a crunchy texture when cooked and work equally well in savory and sweet dishes.

Nutritional Info (per 1-oz serving): *Calories: 120, Sodium: 19 mg, Dietary Fiber: 2.5 g, Total Fat: 7.6 g, Total Carbs: 9.9 g, Protein: 4.2 g.*

Ingredients:

1 apple, peeled, cored and diced

1 cup sprouted wheat berries

½ cup flax seeds, ground

½ cup diced raw walnuts

½ cup millet flour

1 cup sunflower seeds

1 tsp. cinnamon

¼ tsp. salt

¼ cup coconut oil, melted

¼ cup maple syrup

3 Tbsp. apple juice

Instructions:

- Combine apple, wheat berries, flax seeds, walnuts, flour, seeds, cinnamon and salt.
- Blend coconut oil, maple syrup and apple juice with a whisk.

- Add dry ingredients to wet ingredients and stir thoroughly.
- Dehydrate at 115 degrees for 18-24 hours. When crispy, break into large pieces.

Almond Cranberry Cookies

These cookies incorporate almond pulp, which is a by-product of almond milk. Almond pulp is a very adaptable ingredient and can be used in numerous recipes and preparations, such as crackers, breads, crusts and cookies. It can also be dehydrated to be ground into a flour.

Nutritional Info (per 1-oz serving): *Calories: 91, Sodium: 2 mg, Dietary Fiber: 2.3 g, Total Fat: 7.6 g, Total Carbs: 4.8 g, Protein: 2 g.*

Ingredients:

Wet pulp from almond milk

1 banana

2 Tbsp. coconut oil

¾ cup shredded coconut flakes

½ cup dried cranberries

1 Tbsp. honey

½ cup almonds, coarsely chopped

Instructions:

- Place almond pulp, banana and coconut oil in food processor.
- Mix remainder of ingredients and add to the almond pulp mixture.
- Place a small scoop of dough on dehydrator sheets and flatten into a cookie.
- Set temperature to 105 degrees and dehydrate for 10 hours or more.
- Set temperature to 105 degrees and dehydrate for 10 hours or more.

Asian-Inspired Nuts

There are endless varieties of flavor combinations to dress up nuts. These are inspired by Asian ingredients and taste great as a garnish to all kinds of Asian noodle dishes and salads.

Nutritional Info (per 1-oz serving): *Calories: 152, Sodium: 5 mg, Dietary Fiber: 2.3 g, Total Fat: 13.1 g, Total Carbs: 4.4 g, Protein: 6.9 g.*

Ingredients:

16 ounce jar of roasted peanuts

1/3 cup soy sauce

¼ cup water

1 ½ tsp. sesame oil

½ tsp. five spice powder

¼ tsp. ground ginger

Instructions:

- Place nuts in a bowl. Combine all other ingredients and whisk together.
- Pour over nuts. Marinate nuts at least 8 hours or overnight.
- Drain liquid and place nuts on dehydrator tray. Dehydrate for 5 hours at 135 degrees.

Apple Cinnamon Graham Cookies

A slightly sweeter version of ordinary graham crackers, the apple cinnamon variety has the inviting and familiar flavors of apple, honey and cinnamon. If you soak nuts or seeds and don't plan on using them that day or the next day, place them in the refrigerator. Always consume them within 1-2 days after soaking.

Nutritional Info (per 1-oz serving): Calories: 160, Sodium: 2 mg, Dietary Fiber: 3.5 g, Total Fat: 13.3 g, Total Carbs: 6.8 g, Protein: 5.1 g.

Ingredients:

1 cup cashews, soaked for 1 hour

1 cup pecans, soaked for 1 hour

6 cups ground almonds

2 apples, peeled, cored and chopped

1 pear, peeled, cored and chopped

1 cup almond butter

1 ½ cups flax seed

½ cup honey

1 Tbsp. cinnamon

½ tsp. nutmeg

Pinch of salt

Instructions:

- After nuts have been soaked, drain and rinse them.
- Pulse cashews and pecans in food processor until small crumbs form. Add the ground almonds and place in a bowl.

- In the food processor, combine apples, pear, almond butter, flax seed, honey, cinnamon, nutmeg and salt. Add the ground nuts.

- Spread mixture on dehydrator trays, about ¼ inch thick, to the edges.

- Dehydrate 6-8 hours at 115 degrees. Flip over and cut into squares. Continue dehydrating for 6-8 hours or until crunchy.

Banana Breakfast Crepes

These simple, light and airy crepes are a great vehicle for your favorite fillings and toppings. Whip up cream or top with fresh strawberry jam. To achieve a perfect circular shape, once the crepe is fully dehydrated, use a pot lid to trace a circle and a sharp paring knife to slice it out.

Nutritional Info (per 1-oz serving): *Calories: 48, Sodium: 1 mg, Dietary Fiber: 1.6 g, Total Fat: 2 g, Total Carbs: 6.6 g, Protein: 1.2 g.*

Ingredients:

> 2 medium size ripe bananas
>
> 1 tsp. ground flax seed
>
> 1 tsp. almond meal
>
> 1 tsp. almond milk
>
> Dash of cinnamon

Instructions:

- Place all ingredients in a food processor and blend into a liquid.

- Line 2 dehydrator sheets and pour mixture onto them. Liquid should only be about 1/8 inches in thickness. Spread with a spatula.

- Dehydrate at 115 degrees for 3 hours. Crepes should be totally smooth. Do not remove crepes early or they will not hold their shape. Cut into crepe-sized circles.

Basic "Soaked Nuts"

There is research to suggest that first soaking and then drying nuts makes them easier to digest by reducing naturally occurring enzyme inhibitors. This process is referred to as making "crispy nuts" and is generally deemed to be more healthful than eating raw nuts. This is a basic recipe for soaking nuts. Of course, any nut, or a combination thereof, can be used. Cashews, however, are not truly "raw" and do not need to be soaked for longer than 6 hours.

Ingredients:

Nuts, in any quantity and variety

Sea salt, approximately 1 Tbsp. per every 4 cups of nuts

Filtered water (to cover the nuts)

Instructions:

- Combine nuts, sea salt and water in a glass bowl. Cover with a lid or plate and place in a warm location for 12 hours.

- Remove lid and rinse nuts in a colander.

- Spread nuts in a single layer on dehydrator trays for 12-24 hours at 105-150 degrees.

Blueberry Nut Bars

These healthy, portable breakfast bars can be made with dozens of different ingredient combinations. Try substituting strawberries, cherries, raspberries, apples or peaches for the blueberries or try a combination of these fruits.

Nutritional Info (per 1-oz serving): *Calories: 160, Sodium: 0 mg, Dietary Fiber: 2.3 g, Total Fat: 15.4 g, Total Carbs: 3.8 g, Protein: 4.4 g.*

Ingredients:

    1 cup pecans

    1 cup walnuts

    ½ cup almond meal

    3 cups blueberries

Instructions:

- In a food processor, grind pecan and walnuts. Pour into a bowl.
- Place blueberries in food processor and add ground almonds and a little water.
- Mix together blueberries and ground nuts.
- Spread mixture onto dehydrator tray and spread it up to 1 inch thick. Dehydrate for 10 hours at 140 degrees, then flip bars over and dehydrate another 10 hours. When ready, cut into 18-20 bars.

Blueberry Oat Pancakes

If you are on a raw or gluten-free diet, these pancakes prove you can still indulge in delicious breakfast foods! This recipe is not nut-based so it tastes a bit more like a "regular" pancake. You can substitute raspberries or strawberries if you prefer.

Nutritional Info (per 1-oz serving): *Calories: 118, Sodium: 4 mg, Dietary Fiber: 5 g, Total Fat: 5.3 g, Total Carbs: 11.5 g, Protein: 3.9 g.*

Ingredients:

½ cup oat flour

1 cup flax seeds (whole)

3 Tbsp. coconut oil, melted

¼ cup agave nectar

½ cup water

1 Tbsp. vanilla

1 ½ cups fresh blueberries

Instructions:

- Stir ingredients in a large bowl. Be careful not to break up blueberries.

- Set dehydrator to 140 degrees. Dehydrate for 1 hour, flip and dehydrate for 1-2 more hours at 115 degrees.

Caramelized Almonds

Caramelized almonds are a tasty snack on their own, but when used as a topping for green or grain salads, they add a totally new flavor dimension and texture. This recipe works well with many different kinds of nuts, but almonds are especially nutritious. When adding an ingredient such as maple syrup or honey, the nuts will feel sticky when taken out of the dehydrator. Once they are cooled, the mixture will adhere and the nuts will be crispy.

Nutritional Info (per 1-oz serving): Calories: 115, Sodium: 1 mg, Dietary Fiber: 2 g, Total Fat: 8.1 g, Total Carbs: 8.9 g, Protein: 3.4 g.

Ingredients:

1 cup raw almonds

1 cup maple syrup

Sea salt

Instructions:

- In a bowl, mix maple syrup and salt. The mixture should have a salty finish without being too overpowering.
- Coat nuts in maple syrup mixture.
- Place on dehydrator sheets for 8 hours at 95-100 degrees. After 4 hours, turn almonds and continue to dehydrate.

Chocolate Covered Walnuts

These chocolate covered walnuts are sure to satisfy your sweet tooth! For any recipe containing honey as an ingredient, it is important to use non-stick drying sheets. Excalibur ParaFlexx drying sheets are particularly good for fruit leathers and any other sticky recipes. They are easy to clean and re-useable for years.

Nutritional Info (per 1-oz serving): *Calories: 149, Sodium: 95 mg, Dietary Fiber: 2.2 g, Total Fat: 13.7 g, Total Carbs: 4.7 g, Protein: 5.8 g.*

Ingredients:

- 2 cups raw walnuts, soaked overnight
- 2 Tbsp. coconut oil, melted
- 3 Tbsp. cocoa powder
- 1 tsp. flaky sea salt
- 1/2 tsp. cinnamon
- ¼ cup honey or maple syrup

Instructions:

- Drain walnuts and dry. Mix remaining ingredients and pour over walnuts.
- Place on dehydrator sheets for 4 hours at 125 degrees, or until no longer wet or sticky.

Classic Oatmeal Raisin Cookies

If you want a classic oatmeal cookie without the white flour, this is a great starter recipe. If the dough is too dry, you can add water, coconut milk or almond milk to moisten to the right consistency. Dehydrate raisins and dates first to make them easier to blend. If you like your cookies on the softer side, leave them in the dehydrator for the maximum amount of time.

Nutritional Info (per 1-oz serving): *Calories: 101, Sodium: 0 mg, Dietary Fiber: 2.4 g, Total Fat: 1.6 g, Total Carbs: 18.9 g, Protein: 3.9 g.*

Ingredients:

2 cups of oat groats, ground into flour

1 banana

½ cup raisins

¼ tsp. cinnamon

1/8 tsp. nutmeg

3 Tbsp. coconut oil

Instructions:

- In a food processor, blend ingredients until you have a thick, sticky dough.
- Scoop dough by the Tbsp. onto dehydrator sheet for 6-24 hours at 115 degrees.

Coconut Butter Macaroons

These treats have an intense coconut flavor from the coconut butter and shredded coconut. Choose finely shredded coconut rather than the coarser variety for these macaroons. Make sure to top with Himalayan salt, which has a beautiful pink color and a pleasant texture.

Nutritional Info (per 1-oz serving): *Calories: 95, Sodium: 3 mg, Dietary Fiber: 1.3 g, Total Fat: 4 g, Total Carbs: 13.8 g, Protein: 1.4 g.*

Ingredients:

3 cups shredded coconut

¾ cup maple syrup

1 ½ tsp. vanilla extract

½ cup cashew flour

2 cups finely shredded coconut

¼ tsp. Himalayan salt

Instructions:

- Process 3 cups shredded coconut in the food processor until creamy.
- Mix coconut butter, maple syrup, vanilla extract, cashew flour and 2 cups finely shredded coconut in a bowl.
- Using a scooper, scoop Tbsp. onto dehydrator sheet. Sprinkle with salt.
- Dehydrate for 24-30 hours at 110 degrees.

Flax Seed Crackers

Flax seed crackers are a delicious addition to your buffet. They are perfect as an accompaniment for hummus, guacamole or any vegetable dip. If you prefer a crispy cracker, dehydrate these crackers for the maximum times indicated below. If you take crackers out of the dehydrator sooner, you will get a chewier, more pliable cracker.

Nutritional Info (per 1-oz serving): *Calories: 133, Sodium: 7 mg, Dietary Fiber: 6.5 g, Total Fat: 8.2 g, Total Carbs: 7.1 g, Protein: 4.6 g.*

Ingredients:

2 cups flaxseeds

2 cups water

¼ cup low sodium soy sauce

2 Tbsp. sesame seeds

Sea salt and black pepper, to taste

1 ½ Tbsp. fresh lime juice

Instructions:

- Cover flax seeds with water and soak for 1-2 hours. Mixture should be gooey, but not too thin. Add more water to achieve this texture.
- Stir in the remainder of the ingredients.
- Spread the mixture about 1/8 inch thick on dehydrator sheets.
- Set the temperature to 105-115 degrees and dehydrate 4-6 hours. Flip over mixture and dehydrate another 4-6 hours. Break crackers into large pieces after dehydrating.

Fruit n' Nut Balls

These fruit n' nut balls are a delicious, healthy alternative to processed sweets full of refined sugar and added fats. Best of all they are a cinch to prepare and easy to transport wherever you go.

Nutritional Info (per 1-oz serving): *Calories: 102, Sodium: 2 mg, Dietary Fiber: 2.3 g, Total Fat: 8.4 g, Total Carbs: 6.9 g, Protein: 2 g.*

Ingredients:

½ cup dried dates

½ cup figs

½ cup dried cherries

½ cup dried apricots

½ cup dried cranberries

1 cup crushed pecans

1 cup crushed almonds

3 tsp. coconut oil, melted

1 cup flaked coconut

Instructions:

- Finely process dates, figs, cherries, apricots and cranberries in a food processor. Mix with nuts and coconut oil in a bowl.
- Shape into 1" balls and roll balls in coconut.
- Place in dehydrator at 135 degrees for 6 hours.

Fruit & Nut Clusters

This mixture is fairly messy so using teflex non-stick sheets is recommended. You can substitute parchment paper for the teflex, but do not use wax paper, as it will stick to the ingredients. For this recipe, removing the clusters halfway through and placing them on mesh sheet speeds the drying time.

Nutritional Info (per 1-oz serving): *Calories: 110, Sodium: 37 mg, Dietary Fiber: 1.6 g, Total Fat: 7.9 g, Total Carbs: 9.2 g, Protein: 2.8 g.*

Ingredients:

½ cup cashew butter

½ cup maple syrup

1 ½ tsp. cinnamon

1 tsp. salt

1 tsp. vanilla extract

8 dates, pitted

2 cups cashews

1 cup pecans

1 cup dried cranberries

1 cup dried blueberries

1 cup rolled oats, raw

Instructions:

- In a food processor, combine cashew butter, maple syrup, cinnamon, salt, vanilla extract and dates. Pulse until the mixture is smooth.

- In a bowl, combine cashews, pecans, dried fruits and oats. Pour liquid mixture on top and toss to coat.

- Pour batter onto dehydrator sheets and dehydrate for 1 hour at 145 degrees. Reduce temperature to 115 degrees and continue dehydrating for up to 24 hours.

"Graham Crackers"

These crackers have all the flavor of your favorite cookie, but are made primarily of nut flours. You can add any combination of diced nuts, dried fruits or cacao nibs for added texture. If you purchase your almonds or oats whole, ground them first to a powder in a food processor, or preferably a Vitamix.

Nutritional Info (per 1-oz serving): Calories: 142, Sodium: 7 mg, Dietary Fiber: 3.2 g, Total Fat: 10.2 g, Total Carbs: 9.6 g, Protein: 5 g.

Ingredients:

4 cups almond flour

1 cup oat flour

½ cup flax seeds

½ cup almond milk

1 cup maple syrup

1 Tbsp. vanilla

1 Tbsp. cinnamon

Instructions:

- Pulse all ingredients in the food processor.
- Spread onto dehydrator trays. Make sure graham cracker mixture is about 1/8 inch thick. Dehydrate at 115 degrees for 4 hours.
- Cut into squares and then flip and dehydrate for 6 more hours.

Macadamia-Sage Crackers

Macadamia nuts, like other nuts, can be ground to be incorporated into a cracker or cookie. They are a little more expensive than other nuts but you will appreciate the naturally sweet, buttery flavor they lend to any recipe.

Nutritional Info (per 1-oz serving): *Calories: 176, Sodium: 1 mg, Dietary Fiber: 6.4 g, Total Fat: 15.1 g, Total Carbs: 7.2 g, Protein: 4.2 g.*

Ingredients:

2 cups macadamia nuts

2 cups chia or flax seeds

1 ½ Tbsp. fresh sage, crushed

Sea salt and white pepper to taste

3 cups water

½ cup olive oil

Instructions:

- Place macadamia nuts and flax seeds into a food processor and grind into a flour. Add sage, salt and pepper. Process until you have a fine texture.

- In a large bowl, add water to nut and seed mix and stir until thick. Don't pour all the water at once. Add small amounts until a soft dough forms.

- Spread onto dehydrator sheets. Drizzle with olive oil and sprinkle additional sea salt.

- Dehydrate at 110 degrees for 4 hours. Score the crackers, flip them over and dehydrate another 8 hours.

THE COMPLETE FOOD DEHYDRATOR COOKBOOK

Hazelnut Lemon Crackers

Enjoy the interesting combination of hazelnuts and lemon zest in this unusual cracker. Using chia seeds rather than flax seeds produces a crunchier cracker with a lighter taste. If you are incorporating flax, be sure to buy fresh flax seeds to avoid a strong aftertaste. Some recipes, like this one, start the dehydration process at a high temperature for a short time and then reduce the temperature for the remainder of the cooking process. At the higher temperature, the food emits water and remains cool. This method conserves time and also prevents possible fermentation.

Nutritional Info (per 1-oz serving): *Calories: 169, Sodium: 31 mg, Dietary Fiber: 3.7 g, Total Fat: 15.6 g, Total Carbs: 5.5 g, Protein: 4.4 g.*

Ingredients:

½ cup chia seeds

1 cup water

3 cups hazelnuts, soaked overnight, skins removed

1 ½ Tbsp. lemon zest

1 Tbsp. maple syrup

½ tsp. sea salt

Black pepper to taste

Instructions:

- Mix chia seeds in 1 cup water and allow to soften.
- Remove soaked hazelnuts and drain them. Place hazelnuts in food processor and grind until fine.
- Pour ground nuts into a bowl and combine with chia seeds, lemon zest, maple syrup, salt and pepper.
- Spread onto dehydrator trays. Use a spatula to flatten dough to approximately ¼ inch thick. Dehydrate at 145

degrees for 1 hour. Decrease heat to 115 and continue to dehydrate for 8 hours.

Mint-Scented Chocolate Chip Cookies

This recipe substitutes cacao nibs for chocolate chips to create a wonderful raw chocolate chip cookie. Cacao nibs are chocolate in its purest form. They impart an intense chocolate flavor and resemble roasted coffee beans in texture.

Nutritional Info (per 1-oz serving): *Calories: 140, Sodium: 25 mg, Dietary Fiber: 4.7 g, Total Fat: 12.1 g, Total Carbs: 8.8 g, Protein: 4.3 g.*

Ingredients:

1 ½ cups almond meal

1 ½ cups ground pecans

1 cup cocoa powder

¼ cup cacao nibs

½ cup maple syrup

3 Tbsp. coconut oil

1 tsp. peppermint extract

1 tsp. vanilla extract

1 Tbsp. almond milk

½ tsp. salt

Instructions:

- Place all ingredients in food processor and pulse until combined. Ingredients should form a cohesive dough.
- Roll out dough to about ¼ inch thickness.
- Cut out circles using a small glass. Alternatively, skip this process, roll dough into balls and flatten into disks.
- Dehydrate for 24 hours at 115 degrees.

Orange-Scented Granola with Dried Blueberries

Use either soaked buckwheat or oat groats in this recipe, or half of each for variation. Raw buckwheat is kasha in its processed form. The citrus elements add freshness to this granola. While any dried fruit can be used, dried blueberries are a pleasant change from apricots or cranberries.

Nutritional Info (per 1-oz serving): *Calories: 85, Sodium: 0 mg, Dietary Fiber: 2 g, Total Fat: 0.7 g, Total Carbs: 17.4 g, Protein: 2.2 g.*

Ingredients:

2 cups raw buckwheat or oat groats

1 cup dates, pitted

1 cup freshly squeezed orange juice

1 orange, juiced

1 tsp. almond extract

1 tsp. lemon juice

½ cup dried blueberries

Instructions:

- Soak the groats in water and drain after about 1 hour. Rinse well and drain again. Transfer them to a small bowl.

- In a food processor, pulse all other ingredients except dried blueberries until a paste forms. Blend this mixture with the groats. Mix thoroughly.

- Spread mixture on dehydrator sheets. Dehydrate for 12 hours at 115 degrees and flip over. Dehydrate for another 12-15 hours until granola is crispy.

- After dehydrated, crumble granola into bite size pieces and add dried blueberries.

Parmesan Black Pepper Flax Crackers

When making crackers in your dehydrator, the best method for spreading is putting the mixture on one end of the tray and spreading it across in a uniform direction with an offset spatula. If you don't carefully spread the dough, you will end up with crackers of different sizes.

Nutritional Info (per 1-oz serving): *Calories: 131, Sodium: 214 mg, Dietary Fiber: 6.4 g, Total Fat: 7.8 g, Total Carbs: 7.1 g, Protein: 5.2 g.*

Ingredients:

1 cup flax seeds

1 cup water

¼ cup parmesan cheese

½ Tbsp. black pepper

1 clove garlic

1 tsp. flaky sea salt

Instructions:

- Stir all ingredients in a large bowl until it forms a gelatinous dough.

- Spread onto dehydrator sheets so that mixture is about ¼ inch thick. Slice the dough into squares.

- Set temperature to 145 degrees and dehydrate for 30-45 minutes. Reduce temperature to 115 degrees and after 6 hours, flip the crackers.

- Continue dehydrating for 12-18 hours. Crackers should be crispy when ready.

Pepita Crackers

Pepitas, or pumpkin seeds, are highly nutritious. Pepitas may refer to either the hulled kernel or unhulled seed that has been roasted. Pumpkin seeds are full of magnesium, B vitamins and protein. Packed in this savory cracker, the roasted flavor of the pepitas makes for a crunchy and satisfying snack.

Nutritional Info (per 1-oz serving): *Calories: 107, Sodium: 2 mg, Dietary Fiber: 3.3 g, Total Fat: 4.3 g, Total Carbs: 14.9 g, Protein: 4.5 g.*

Ingredients:

2 ½ cups sprouted quinoa

¾ cup chia seeds, finely ground

¼ cup low sodium soy sauce

2 cloves garlic

1 tsp. onion powder

½ tsp. salt

½ cup pepitas

Instructions:

- Process quinoa until finely ground. Add all the other ingredients except pepitas and pulse until well combined.
- Spread mixture on dehydrator sheets. Sprinkle pepitas on top and press down to adhere to mixture.
- Cut into squares. Dehydrate for 8-12 hours at 140 degrees or until crunchy.

"Raw" Cheesy Thyme Crackers

With all the flavor of a cheese cracker from nutritional yeast and the addition of fresh herbs, you will fall in love with these raw crackers. And unlike many other raw food recipes, these crackers have just 5 ingredients, which makes for easy preparation and quick cleanup.

Nutritional Info (per 1-oz serving): *Calories: 132, Sodium: 37 mg, Dietary Fiber: 4.5 g, Total Fat: 10.4 g, Total Carbs: 7.2 g, Protein: 5.5 g.*

Ingredients:

2 cups almonds, soaked overnight and dried

4 Tbsp. ground chia seeds

4 Tbsp. nutritional yeast

2 ½ Tbsp. fresh thyme, chopped

½ tsp. salt

Instructions:

- Soak chia seeds in ½ cup of water for 30 minutes. Drain.
- Place almonds, chia seeds, nutritional yeast, thyme and salt in a food processor. Pulse several times.
- Add a few drops of water while motor is running until mixture becomes spreadable.
- Spread mixture onto dehydrator sheets and set temperature to 115 degrees. Dehydrate for 4-6 hours. Flip over and cut into cracker shapes. Dehydrate another 8 hours.

"Raw" Granola

You can use your dehydrator to dehydrate nuts and seeds to create hundreds of variations of this basic granola recipe. Granola will stay crunchy if stored correctly. See Chapter 7, Dehydrating and Storing Safely, for additional storage tips.

Nutritional Info (per 1-oz serving): *Calories: 131, Sodium: 7 mg, Dietary Fiber: 2.3 g, Total Fat: 7.8 g, Total Carbs: 12.1 g, Protein: 4.7 g.*

Ingredients:

  3 cups rolled oats

  ¼ cup oat bran

  1 cup raw pumpkin seeds

  1 cup raw sunflower seeds

  1 cup coconut

  1 cup walnuts, pecans or almonds

  ½ cup honey

  ½ cup coconut oil, melted

  ½ cup water

  1 tsp. cinnamon

  ¼ tsp. nutmeg

Instructions:

- Mix together honey, oil and water. Add all the remaining ingredients.
- Spread mixture onto dehydrator sheets and smooth to create a thin layer.
- Dehydrate for 18 hours at 105-115 degrees.

Savory Onion and Garlic Crisps

You can create bold flavors with just a few ingredients as this recipe demonstrates. If you do not like raw garlic, use minced dried garlic from the pantry. Vidalia onions contribute a sweet note to this savory crisp.

Nutritional Info (per 1-oz serving): *Calories: 116, Sodium: 4 mg, Dietary Fiber: 7.7 g, Total Fat: 8.1 g, Total Carbs: 8.9 g, Protein: 4.9 g.*

Ingredients:

1 Vidalia onion, peeled and halved

2 cloves garlic, peeled and ground

1 cup ground flax seeds

1 cup ground chia seeds

1 ½ cups ground sunflower seeds

½ cup low sodium soy sauce

½ cup extra virgin olive oil

½ tsp. white pepper

Instructions:

- Place onions and garlic in food processor and process roughly, but do not create a paste.
- Transfer to a mixing bowl and add all other ingredients. Mix until combined.
- Spread mixture on dehydrator sheet and dehydrate at 100 degrees for 24-36 hours.
- After dehydrating, cut into large squares.

Savory Trail Mix

Savory trail mix is a departure from your traditional sweet blends. Raw nuts are combined with a low sodium soy sauce and spices to give you a new granola experience.

Nutritional Info (per 1-oz serving): *Calories: 120, Sodium: 19 mg, Dietary Fiber: 2.5 g, Total Fat: 7.6 g, Total Carbs: 9.9 g, Protein: 4.2 g.*

Ingredients:

1 cup raw almonds, soaked overnight and dried

1 cup raw pumpkin seeds, soaked overnight and dried

1 cup raw sunflower seeds, soaked overnight and dried

3 Tbsp. low sodium soy sauce

3 Tbsp. olive oil

1 tsp. garlic powder

2 tsp. onion powder

½ tsp. celery salt

Pinch of cayenne pepper

Instructions:

- Combine soy sauce, olive oil and seasonings. Pour onto nuts and seeds and stir until they are well coated.
- Spread mixture onto dehydrator tray using mesh sheets.
- Dehydrate for 18 hours at 105-115 degrees.

Seasoned Sunflower Seeds

When dehydrating nuts and seeds, you should try to keep the temperature around 110 degrees to preserve the greatest amount of natural enzymes and unsaturated fatty acids. Don't exceed 150 degrees, which is the temperature at which these elements start to break down.

Nutritional Info (per 1-oz serving): *Calories: 140, Sodium: 3 mg, Dietary Fiber: 2.1 g, Total Fat: 12.3 g, Total Carbs: 5 g, Protein: 5 g.*

Ingredients:

2 Tbsp. olive oil

1 Tbsp. soy sauce

½ tsp. garlic powder

½ tsp. onion powder

½ tsp. celery salt

¼ tsp. crushed red pepper flakes

2 cups shelled sunflower seeds, raw

Instructions:

- Soak sunflower seeds overnight. Rinse and dry thoroughly.
- Mix together the olive oil, soy sauce and seasonings. Toss seeds in the mixture until they are well coated.
- Place on a dehydrator tray and dehydrate for 12-18 hours at 105-115 degrees.

Sesame Seed Crisps

These sesame seed crisps are a great option for anyone with a nut allergy. They do not contain any nut butters or ground nuts. With no added oils, they are also a healthy and low-fat alternative to store-bought and many homemade crackers.

Nutritional Info (per 1-oz serving): *Calories: 147, Sodium: 71 mg, Dietary Fiber: 4.5 g, Total Fat: 11.4 g, Total Carbs: 6.8 g, Protein: 4.8 g.*

Ingredients:

½ cup flax seeds

1 cup water

½ cup sesame seeds, toasted

½ cup black sesame seeds

½ tsp. sea salt

½ tsp. dried thyme

½ tsp. garlic powder

Instructions:

- In a bowl, mix seeds and seasonings with water. Stir until the mixture is well incorporated and leave for 10-15 minutes to allow seeds to become pudding-like.

- Spread onto dehydrator trays. Batter should be less than ¼ inch thick. Dehydrate at 110 degrees for 8-12 hours. Flip them over and dehydrate for another 8 hours.

Spicy Cashews

If you like heat, these nuts are for you! You can adjust the amount of chili powder and hot sauce to your tastes. The addition of lime juice supplies a fresh note and balances the heat.

Nutritional Info (per 1-oz serving): *Calories: 148, Sodium: 68 mg, Dietary Fiber: 1.5 g, Total Fat: 11.8 g, Total Carbs: 9.3 g, Protein: 4 g.*

Ingredients:

16 ounce jar of roasted cashews

½ cup water

¼ cup hot sauce

1 ½ Tbsp. chili powder

¼ cayenne pepper

3 Tbsp. fresh lime juice

1 lime, zested

Instructions:

- Place nuts in a bowl. Combine all other ingredients and whisk together.
- Pour over nuts. Marinate nuts at least 8 hours or overnight.
- Drain liquid and place nuts on dehydrator tray. Dehydrate for 5 hours at 135 degrees.

Sweet and Salty Pumpkin Seeds

These pumpkin seeds are great as part of a trail mix or in your breakfast cereal. This recipe soaks overnight and then gets additional flavor from the addition of turmeric and ginger. You can also try this preparation with sunflower seeds.

Nutritional Info (per 1-oz serving): *Calories: 131, Sodium: 5 mg, Dietary Fiber: 1.3 g, Total Fat: 10.6 g, Total Carbs: 5.8 g, Protein: 5.7 g.*

Ingredients:

2 cups pumpkin seeds

2 Tbsp. olive oil

1 Tbsp. paprika

1 Tbsp. turmeric

1 Tbsp. sugar

1 tsp. ground ginger

Instructions:

- Soak pumpkin seeds overnight in enough water to cover the seeds.
- Dry seeds and mix remaining ingredients. Toss seeds in the mixture until they are well coated.
- Place on a dehydrator tray.
- Dehydrate for 12-18 hours at 105-115 degrees.

Sweet Cocoa Chia Bars

Chia seeds are full of omega-3 fatty acids, which have be found to support brain health. They are a great source of fiber and have been linked to improving blood pressure in diabetics and lowering cholesterol. These cocoa crisps are a great way to get the health benefits of chia seeds in a raw "chocolate bar." When spreading mixture, use one tray for a thicker cookie/cracker and 2 trays for a thinner consistency.

Nutritional Info (per 1-oz serving): Calories: 125, Sodium: 32 mg, Dietary Fiber: 6 g, Total Fat: 9.6 g, Total Carbs: 5.6 g, Protein: 5.2 g.

Ingredients:

1 cup chia seeds

2 cups water

¼ cup cocoa powder

6 figs, chopped

1 apple, peeled, cored and chopped

1 cup walnuts, chopped

3 Tbsp. honey

3 Tbsp. cacao nibs

Instructions:

- Soak chia seeds in ½ cup of water for 30 minutes. Drain.
- Blend all remaining ingredients in a blender, except for cacao nibs. Add small amounts of water to achieve the right consistency.
- Stir together chia seeds, blended mixture and cacao nibs.
- Allow to rest for 20-25 minutes.
- Spread the mixture onto dehydrator tray. Dehydrate for 1 hour at 135 degrees. Cut into bars.

- Lower temperature to 110 degrees and dehydrate another 8 hours. Flip bars and dehydrate another 8 hours.

Wasabi Sesame Crackers

Undiluted wasabi powder has a very sharp flavor so a little goes a long way. It is preferable to mix wasabi powder into a paste before using it as an ingredient. Combine equal amounts of wasabi powder and water and combine until well incorporated. Let mixture rest for 10 minutes to allow flavor to develop.

Nutritional Info (per 1-oz serving): *Calories: 169, Sodium: 1 mg, Dietary Fiber: 3.5 g, Total Fat: 15 g, Total Carbs: 5.9 g, Protein: 4.3 g.*

Ingredients:

2 cups hazelnut meal

¼ cup toasted sesame seeds

1/3 cup black sesame seeds

¼ cup chia seeds

2 Tbsp. wasabi powder (mixed with water to form a paste)

½ cup water

1 tsp. soy sauce

1 Tbsp. sesame oil

1 Tbsp. olive oil

1 Tbsp. toasted sesame oil

Instructions:

- Combine hazelnut meal, sesame seeds and chia seeds.
- In a small bowl, whisk wasabi mixture, water, soy sauce and oils.
- Pour wet ingredients into dry ingredients to form a dough.
- Using a cookie scoop, scoop dough and place on the mesh dehydrator sheet. Flatten the ball to form a circular shape.

- Dehydrate for 8-10 hours at 110 degrees.

Sundried Tomato Flax Crackers

Flax seeds are the richest plant source of omega-3 essential fatty acids. Flax seeds are endlessly versatile as the base for a variety of raw crackers. Using the basic 1:1 ratio of flax seeds to water, you can create many different flavor combinations. This recipe pairs traditional Italian flavors of tomatoes, basil and thyme.

Nutritional Info (per 1-oz serving): *Calories: 120, Sodium: 232 mg, Dietary Fiber: 6.4 g, Total Fat: 6.7 g, Total Carbs: 8.2 g, Protein: 4.4 g.*

Ingredients:

1 cup flax seeds

1 cup water

1 Tbsp. dried basil

½ Tbsp. dried thyme

2 Tbsp. sundried tomatoes, ground

1 Tbsp. extra-virgin olive oil

1 tsp. flaky sea salt

Instructions:

- Stir all ingredients, except salt, in a large bowl until it forms a gelatinous mass. This should take about an hour.

- Spread onto dehydrator sheets so that mixture is about 1/8 inch – ¼ inch thick. Sprinkle with sea salt.

- Set temperature to 105 degrees and dehydrate for 4 hours. Flip and score the mixture.

- Continue dehydrating for 6-10 hours.

NEXT STEPS...

DID YOU ENJOY THIS BOOK?

IF SO, THEN LET ME KNOW BY LEAVING A REVIEW! Reviews are the lifeblood of independent authors, I would appreciate even a few words and rating if that's all you have time for.

IF YOU DID NOT LIKE THIS BOOK, THEN PLEASE TELL ME! Email me at feedback@HHFpress.com and let me know what you didn't like! Perhaps I can change it. In today's world a book doesn't have to be stagnant, it can improve with time and feedback from readers like you. You can impact this book, and I welcome your feedback. Help make this book better for everyone!

ABOUT THE AUTHOR

Lisa Brian is a private chef extraordinaire who has prepared meals and specialty foods and beverages for many celebrities along California's coast, from Los Angeles and San Francisco. She has a background in nutrition, and is a highly trained chef. When she's not writing books, she spends her time developing new recipes and cooking up fresh servings of health and happiness for her clients and her family.

DON'T FORGET TO REGISTER FOR FREE BOOKS...

Every month we release a new book, and we offer it to our current readers first...absolutely free! This helps us get early feedback before launching a book, and lets you stock your shelf full of interesting and valuable books for free!

Some recent titles include:

- The Complete Vegetable Spiralizer Cookbook

- The Cast Iron Recipe Cookbook

- 101 Crepe Recipe

To receive this month's free book, just go to

www.healthyhappyfoodie.org/e1-freebooks

Printed in Great Britain
by Amazon.co.uk, Ltd.,
Marston Gate.